JULIE

ALL MY HOPE

A PRISONER NO MORE

BRIDGE LOGOS

Newberry, FL 32669

Bridge-Logos
Newberry, FL 32669

All My Hope:
A Prisoner No More
by Julie Seals

Printed in the United States of America.

Library of Congress Catalog Card Number: 2023934972

International Standard Book Number: 978-1-61036-162-0

Literary Agent and Editor: L. Edward Hazelbaker
L.Edward@TheWornKeyboard.com

Interior Layout and Cover Design: Ashley Morgan
GraphicGardenLLC@gmail.com

WHAT OTHERS ARE SAYING

Julie's story is a compelling journey of finding freedom in the least likely place—a prison cell! Every page is filled with the evidence of God's relentless pursuit for us even when we're running hard and fast in the opposite direction. My prayer is that this book will reach the multitudes trapped in addiction, shame, and regret. Through her compassionate words, may you find hope, peace and restoration that only Jesus can give. Get ready to see the power of God in action! I believe you will never be the same after encountering Julie's God—the God of the impossible (Matthew 19:26).

—**SUZANNE COX**, Co-founder, Legacy of Purpose

In all my years, I have never known a woman like my extraordinary friend, Julie Seals. To pass this beautiful, friendly, blonde-haired, blue-eyed woman at church, you would never imagine the depth of despair she experienced. But she has also experienced the love of Jesus that took her from drug addiction and prison to a credentialed minister with the Assemblies of God. Because of Julie's courage, resilience, and obedience, her life was completely transformed by the power of God and filled with purpose and vision. Now her mission is bringing hope to the hopeless, from the prisons to the pews. Her story will inspire you to believe that no matter how far you or your loved one has fallen, the redeeming love of God can restore it all.

—**PASTOR NONDA HOUSTON**, National Director,
Assemblies of God Women

When you serve the Lord in ministry for 40 years, hopefully you're going to have seen miracles happening all around you. I'm so grateful to have been the witness to those! Yet, every once in a great while you meet someone like Julie Seals, who persevered against all odds through some of the most unbelievable circumstances, trials, and tribulations. I believe it's a combination of her calling, her faith, and her perseverance that created one of the most compelling and encouraging testimonies I've ever heard. Every time I hear a piece of her story, another of God's incredible examples of his unfailing love comes shining through, and it touches me to the core. My eyes start leaking every single time! Julie and her amazing husband, Mike, share a deep burden for souls who are doing time in prison—a burden like mine. I'm grateful for their friendship, and I'm grateful for their incredible example of tenacity and courage. I'm blessed to be attached to their future!

—**C.J. ORNDORFF, III**, Second Chance TBN Outreach Ministries

---

I want to shout from the rooftops for everyone to read *All My Hope*. To write about hope is one thing; to be a hope dealer is entirely another. This is Julie Seals! Her passion, hunger, faith, and love for Jesus is contagious. She is a burning and shining light in this lost and dying world. Julie found healing for her broken life through Jesus. Now let her help you find yours. It's time for the world to hear her riveting story.

—**REVEREND DR. JAMIE MORGAN**, Mentor to Women in Ministry

Julie Seals—the author of *All My Hope*—inspires me. Julie found herself lying on the floor of a jail cell, having lost everything but her physical life. Her child, her freedom, part of her body, her hope, and her future were all gone. Yet, there was Someone else on that floor—Jesus! Her book is not the inspirational story of Julie's recovery. It is the miraculous record of her re-creation. *All My Hope: A Prisoner No More* documents God's restoration of all the devil stole from her. Today, Julie is a happy wife, an effective ministry leader, an evangelist, a motivational speaker, and an inspiration to her son and her husband—and to *me*. Read this book. Rejoice with Julie in her hope, her freedom, and how far she has come from that filthy floor. She is a prisoner NO MORE!

—**REVEREND DR. TERRY RABURN**, Superintendent, PenFlorida District of the Assemblies of God

---

The book you are holding in your hands is a rare and beautiful treasure. Still, I encourage you to read it with a box of tissue close at hand. I cried tears of sadness and tears of joy as I envisioned the heart-wrenching journey of Julie's life unfolding before me. Julie takes us from miracle to miracle in her story as she proves over and over again that Our God is truly capable of meeting our every need. Through all of her despair, struggle, and loss, God's mighty hand provided, protected, and prepared the way before her. As a prison minister myself, I know this book will turn the lives of the incarcerated upside down with hope and encouragement. I believe Julie will see much fruit from her labor through this book, and I also see this as a great inspiration for the families of incarcerated individuals. I believe anyone who reads this book will be inspired while reading of Julie's growing relationship with God. It causes us to look at our own journeys with God and remember those intimate moments of coming to know Him, and it reminds us to continue to trust Him with every aspect of our lives. My spirit has been stirred, and I believe you too will be uplifted and find yourself rejoicing with Julie as you come to the end of her breathtaking testimony. All our hope is truly found in having a relationship with Jesus.

—**DONNA SPARKS**, Assemblies of God Evangelist, Author, Prison Minister, and Revivalist

---

Julie Seals is a living, breathing testimony to the grace and power of God! Read this book to be inspired and to know that God is still working His wonders in the earth today!

—**NEAL GORDON**, Pastor, Abundant Life Church, Lebanon, Kentucky

DEDICATION

This book is dedicated to my Lord and Savior, Jesus Christ, who gave me a second chance at life, and to my precious son, Tyler, who gave me a second chance to be his mom.

ACKNOWLEDGMENTS

There are some people without whose love and support this book would never have become a reality. I want to honor and thank each one of them.

To Mike—thank you for trusting God and marrying me, an ex-addict felon, without giving it a second thought. Thank you for going a hundred extra miles to help me find my son, and for never letting me give up along the way. Finally, thank you for your patience over the past six years of my incessant yapping about writing this book!

To my daughter-in-law, Laura—thank you for the instrumental role you played in that first phone call and every moment that followed. You were truly handpicked by God for our family. You are a courageous, kind, strong woman of God, and I couldn't adore you more than I already do.

To Dr. Jamie Morgan—thank you for mentoring me through every step of this process, including the 11:00 PM phone call to help me land the plane and write the final chapter. Without you, this book would still be a half-finished dream instead of a published reality. God knew how much I needed you!

To Susie—thank you for leading me to the Lord, for planting the first seed in my heart, and for praying fervently over so many years for Tyler.

To Nonda and Gordon Houston—thank you for your friendship and influence in our lives. Without that, my story could have had an entirely different outcome. You are both cherished gifts from God.

To Pastors Neal and Dominique Gordon and Abundant Life Church—thank you for your generous love offering that made it possible for me to have *All My Hope* professionally edited. Know that you played no small role in this.

To every person in my life who has believed God with me throughout the years for Tyler to be restored to my life. (There are too many to mention, but you know who you are.)—thank you for praying with me for the realization of God's promise to restore him to me.

To L. Edward Hazelbaker, my Editor and Agent—thank you for believing in my story and in God's vision for *All My Hope*. Thank you for driving eight hours to come see me. And very important to me—thank you for your great sense of humor and for every outburst of uproarious laughter you provided me.

To Bridge-Logos Publishing and its CEO, Suzi Wooldridge—thank you for welcoming me into the Bridge-Logos family, for taking me on as a new author, for loving my story, and for your huge heart to support my ministry. I love you already.

To Don Wilkerson—I have loved the Teen Challenge program and ministry ever since I read *The Cross and The Switchblade* seventeen years ago. To have the foreword of my book written by you is an honor beyond description, for which I am eternally grateful.

To Ashley Morgan—thank you for the most gorgeous cover design that captures my joy and the hope Christ gave to me when He set this prisoner free!

—JULIE SEALS

TABLE OF CONTENTS

FOREWORD

There are some amazing-grace, modern-day stories that need told, and this is one of them. I have seen and heard many such testimonies in my many years working with addicts in Teen Challenge as Co-founder with my late brother, David Wilkerson. I can tell you this one will leave you with undeniable proof of the power of the gospel of Jesus Christ to change a life in a dramatic way.

This life story will grip you, and you will find yourself drawn into it from beginning to end. Chapter by chapter, I found myself captivated by the series of miracles Julie experienced. It is a life account of guilt to grace—from deep darkness to the shining new light of faith—and it is proof that when you walk in obedience to God, His favor and power opens doors that otherwise are closed.

Julie found joy when she found Jesus; or it can be said Jesus found her. Don't miss the heart-wrenching separation from her son and God's power and grace exhibited in her reconciliation with him as a highlight of her book. I pray Julie's story contained in *All My Hope* gets into the hands of other hopeless women and men. May reading this be a Life-Changer for many.

The book is well written, and as the story develops, I hope you will join me in cheering Julie on to a glorious finishing line—the end of her purpose-filled future spoken of by "Tyler" in his introduction.

—**DON WILKERSON**, Co-founder,
Teen Challenge and Times Square Church,
President Emeritus, Teen Challenge, Inc.

INTRODUCTION

This book is a love story about a broken, lost, sinful woman who found Jesus. It's a story of how a perfect, loving Savior lifted her out of darkness, transformed her, and gave her a second chance at life.

Out of respect for those who were part of the dark, out-of-control years of her life, the names used in this story are sometimes fictitious, and some details that could do harm to people from her past have been excluded.

Yes, this is a love story. It's a love story about how the compassionate God of the universe looked down on one outcast of society—a woman who felt worthless, purposeless, hopeless, and utterly broken—and forgave her, loved her, and rescued her from a life of certain destruction.

That woman is Julie Seals!

Jesus lifted her out of the slimy pit—out of the mud and the mire—set her feet upon an indestructible rock, and made her a brand-new person. It is the God of miracles who gave her hope and a purpose-filled future. And I hope you will allow God to do the same for YOU!

Out of all the women I have known in my life, the one who has had the greatest impact on my walk with Jesus has got to be Julie Seals. She is an amazing speaker, leader, wife, and servant of the Living God. She is radically on fire for the Lord and truly walks out her faith.

I was nineteen years old when I met her for the second time, and the love and gratefulness I would like to express to God for putting her in my life would itself take a book to explain.

Julie has been there for me in the darkest times of my life, and I believe it's only because of her prayer and intercession to God on my behalf that I'm alive and living for Him today.

I say all of this to preface in a unique way what you are about to read.

This book will powerfully impact your life if you are willing to open your heart to what God wants to do in you through the author's testimony. And hopefully your hope for the future and your expectation for God to do a miracle in your life will overflow as you come to understand why it is significant that this introduction is written by Julie's son.

My name is Tyler, and THIS is my mom's story!

—**TYLER**

CHAPTER 1

LIFE AS I KNEW IT WAS OVER

MY HEART POUNDED as I let them duct tape four pounds of crystal methamphetamine pressed in flattened plastic bags around my waist. As the tape was being wound around me I stared out the sliding glass door into a cold, grey, rainy day as the distant ocean churned.

Seaweed-filled waves crashed relentlessly upon the sandy shore in front of my rented beach house in Ensenada, Mexico, as in my mind I expressed my uneasiness without speaking to the others.

"God must not have heard my prayer last night," I thought to myself. "He doesn't see me. Nothing has changed. I don't feel any different."

I was thirty-five years old then as I went down the mental checklist of all that went wrong in my life. My left leg had been amputated below the knee. My son had been taken from me. And my beloved dad had died. In addition, I was living as a fugitive in another country, hopelessly strung out with a meth lab in my bathroom.

And without something to prevent it, my remaining foot was also likely soon to be amputated.

Only twelve hours earlier, in the very spot where I was then standing, I had collapsed on the floor as I sobbed and begged God to become the center of my life or I'd be lost forever.

"Perhaps He didn't respond because I'm entrenched in a world of evil," I thought. "Maybe it's too late for me."

The job of preparing me for the drug delivery was completed, and we left on our mission.

The drive to the Mexico/San Ysidro border took about an hour. I shifted nervously in the passenger seat. I was a drug mule, ready to walk across and deliver the meth to a member of a big drug cartel. As I gazed out at the rain through the passenger window of the sleek Camaro, I was struck by the extreme poverty of the Tijuana landscape.

Torn fabric tarps served as roofs for tiny homes with dirt floors and walls made of concrete blocks. Wet laundry hung on sagging clothes lines, and makeshift security systems stood vigil constructed with broken beer bottles cemented on top of crooked concrete block fences.

Suddenly, I heard a voice say, "Julie, this is the last time you're ever going to see this."

My forehead furrowed deeply as I thought, "What was THAT?"

It was not my voice. It wasn't the driver of the car. It wasn't even my thought! I grew nervous. The border was approaching. It was time to get out of the car and walk across.

I didn't want to go through with it.

I stepped nervously out of the car and watched it pull away. I was alone, and something felt terribly wrong. I walked across the street to a Telnor phone booth and called the meth cook.

"I don't want to do this anymore," I said. "I don't feel good about this."

"Just go! Do it. You'll be fine," he reassured me.

I hung up the phone. And it felt like a greater force began propelling me through the pedestrian crossing at the border. As I walked, a female customs officer approached me and asked where I was coming from and what I had been doing in Mexico.

Fear paralyzed me as I mumbled something unintelligible.

She then asked me where my luggage was. My eyes widened, and my tongue stuck to the roof of my mouth.

Glancing toward the open door that led to San Ysidro, I envisioned myself making a run for it. I was only ten feet from freedom. I became lightheaded. My vision grew fuzzy at the edges, and my heart sunk in my chest like a piece of lead.

Moments later I heard myself confessing to the customs officer what I was doing, and I asked if we could go into a private room so I could take the meth off and give it to her.

I was turning myself in!

I held my breath and waited for her to slam me against a wall or throw me on the cement floor and cuff me. I knew my life was over. I lost everything in that final act of desperation. I literally had nothing left to live for.

Then all of a sudden I felt what I now know was the presence of God come over me like an invisible shield, and again I heard *that voice* speak to me inside my head. "Two years, Julie."

I shook my head in disagreement. "If that's God, he must not have realized that four pounds of meth is a life sentence," I thought to myself. Then again, the voice came to me—and insistently—"Two years!"

The customs officer spoke to me softly and guided me down a hallway and into a small, solid concrete room. She never pulled out her handcuffs. She didn't even grab my arm.

A tear slid down my face as I asked her why she was treating me with such kindness.

She explained gently, “Just because you have packages on your person doesn’t mean you don’t deserve to be treated with dignity.”

I had to take off the packages of meth, which was no easy feat. The kind customs officer was not allowed to help me, and I trembled as I tugged at the layers of duct tape. Next, I was taken to speak with a detective, who handcuffed me, read me my rights, and put me in a police car.

Fifteen minutes later, a series of heavy metal doors slammed shut behind me as I was escorted deep into the bowels of the Metropolitan Correctional Center in San Diego, California.

Life as I knew it was over.

MY PURPOSE

Have you been in that place—the place where it was clear that life as you knew it was over? Have you ever come up against seemingly insurmountable obstacles and wondered how you would ever make it to the other side? Perhaps thoughts have gone through your head, such as,

“How did everything go so wrong?”

“There’s no way out of this!”

“I’ve messed up beyond repair!”

“I’ll never recover from this!”

“This mountain is too high to . . . !”

“This valley is too low to . . . !”

“The loss is too great to . . . !”

“I can’t go on!”

“Nothing will ever be the same again!”

If so, this book was written just for you, to stir your faith and flood your soul with HOPE! My prayer is that you will find yourself somewhere within the pages of my story and encounter God in a personal way that forever transforms you.

Within the pages of this book you will discover the love and power of God, and I want you to know that the same love you are going to read about being poured out on me is available to *you*.

God created you to walk in victory and boldly fulfill a unique calling and destiny. Nobody else can do what God created *you* to do. He wants to take your circumstances, your mistakes, and your greatest pain, and turn them into something so incredible that it will blow your mind to see what God does with them.

You see, when it looks like you've hit a dead end—when everything seems to have gone horribly wrong—and when life as you know it seems to come to an end,

God is there!

A new day is coming.

Get ready, my friend.

God has a plan and a purpose for you, and nothing you've done has cancelled that out!

Chapter 2

THE WAR FOR MY SOUL

A BABY GIRL was born at St. John's Hospital in Santa Monica, California, and something was wrong. There was a hole at the base of the baby's spine. And her spinal cord, with a large tumor wrapped around it, was protruding through her skin!

The doctors rushed off with the baby to an operating room, but minutes later one of them brought her back and handed her to her parents, who stared at him expectantly.

"Your baby is going to die," the doctor said. "If she lives, she will be mentally retarded and will never be able to walk."

After questions were asked and answered, the baby's mother spoke from her heart to the doctor. "We're taking her so she can die at home," the young mother managed to say through her tears.

The year was 1965. And the baby . . . was me.

In Psalm 139 we read something David said to God. *"You made all the delicate, inner parts of my body and knit me together in my mother's womb"* (v.13). *"You saw me before I was born. Every day of my life was recorded in your book. Every moment was laid out before a single day had passed"* (v.16).[1]

---

1 Unless otherwise indicated, all Scripture quotations are taken from the Holy Bible, New Living Translation, copyright © 1996, 2004, 2015 by Tyndale House Foundation. Used by permission of Tyndale House Publishers, Carol Stream, Illinois 60188. All rights reserved.

Even before I was born, I was created for a purpose—God's purpose! And He already had a plan for me even though my parents took me home to die.

THE SCARY THING IN OUR HOUSE

I didn't die, of course! Six months later I underwent an operation to remove most of the tumor, and my spinal cord was pushed back inside my body. Miraculously, I walked before I was one year old and was reading a newspaper before I turned three. Nobody told me that I was different from other children, and I certainly didn't look different.

I remember being about four years old when I felt like "someone" was with me and was watching over me. I also knew, even as a little girl, that the *someone* was God. I felt His presence and His goodness, and I knew He loved me.

There was, however, another force active in my parents' home as I was growing up. And that one was not good; it was evil. I remember being a young teenager and seeing a Ouija board in a cupboard. When I asked about it, my mom told me she and my dad used to play with it and ask it a series of questions when I was very little. She said what happened one time, though, scared them both so badly that they stopped instantly and put it away.

My mom explained to me that they invited some friends over to the house when I was about two. They gathered around our heavy, solid wood dining room table and put their hands on the Ouija board while calling out to spirits. Much to their surprise, the table rose off the floor.

My mom said she started mocking whatever it was that made the table levitate. And she said when she did that, the table flew out from beneath everyone's hands and pinned her up against a wall. After that experience, she hid the Ouija board in a cupboard, and after a while, she forgot about it.

I have chills just writing this story. It really happened, and it terrified my parents. They dabbled in things of the spirit world they knew nothing about, and it opened up a door for evil to enter our home.

I grew up in that home in Orange County, California. At the age of four or five, I remember my bedroom light turning on and off by itself. I also remember watching my bedroom door open and close on its own. At that time, I thought it was *Casper the Friendly Ghost*, a popular cartoon character of that era. I loved Casper. Casper was friendly and good, but whatever was in my parents' house was not.

Over the years, as my little sister, Kelly, and I were growing up, there were occasional spurts of inexplicable happenings in our home. On some nights, at approximately three o'clock in the morning, my family was awakened by an unbelievably loud crash! To me it sounded as though someone had picked up a huge wooden piece of furniture, held it up high, and slammed it down on a wooden floor.

But we had a fully carpeted house, and we never found anything that had fallen over or that could have been responsible for that loud crash. On those early mornings when the crash reverberated throughout our house, my sister and I were jolted out of bed, and we ran to the middle of the upstairs hallway balcony.

My parents, too, ran from their downstairs bedroom, and wide-eyed and a little scared, it was common for us all to ask, "What was THAT?"

My dad suggested it was perhaps a sonic boom. That explanation might have sufficed except that more unexplained events continued to happen. Furniture in our home was moving around as we slept.

On several nights, my mom woke up, got out of bed to use the bathroom, and fell on top of the piano bench! It had moved from the entranceway of our home into my mom and dad's bedroom while they slept with the door closed. For many years, Mom blamed Kelly and me for moving the piano bench, but we didn't do it!

ANOTHER OPERATION

When I turned twelve and started to go through adolescence I hit a growth spurt that caused the tumor that was still in my back to pull on my spinal cord. Within a few months, my feet and legs turned purple, green, and black, and I went from walking to crawling around the house.

The pain in my feet and legs became so severe that I curled up in a corner and cried for hours until my mom found me.

Mom then took me to the doctor, and the doctor's diagnosis wasn't good. I needed another surgery on my back. So I went into surgery again, and that time the operation took six hours. And once again the prognosis was that I would never again be able to walk.

But God had a different plan. I went home *walking* after only five days!

THE SEED WAS PLANTED

I was so excited! My older half-sister, Susie, was moving to California to live with us! I always wanted a big sister. Now there would be three of us girls in the family. Over the years, Susie had come to visit on a fairly regular basis, and with each visit it grew harder to say goodbye when she left.

Family was very important to my mother, and she worked with my paternal grandmother to arrange for Susie to fly out from Michigan to visit us. Susie's first visit occurred when I was a baby, and she flew out to spend time with us every year or so thereafter.

I knew Susie was my big sister, and I admired everything about her. Susie was beautiful. She was also smart, funny, tall, and thin. I always wanted a "full-time" big sister, and now it was going to happen! I was ecstatic.

I was fifteen the year Susie moved in with us. She was twenty, and as a brand-new Christian on fire for the Lord, she was eager to share her newfound faith. I remember with great clarity the night she called me into her bedroom to tell me she was worried about my soul. As we sat cross-legged on her bed facing each other, she opened her Bible and read to me the passage in John chapter three, where Jesus said to Nicodemus, "*You must be born again*" (v.7).

I didn't understand any of it, but I could see that Susie really loved me. That weird thing about being *born again* really mattered to her, so to appease her, I let her take my hands in hers and lead me in a sinner's prayer that went something like this:

> "Dear Jesus," I prayed after her, "I know that I am a sinner. I believe that you died for my sins. Please forgive me and come into my heart and save me. Amen."

Although I didn't understand what I was saying or doing, something deep inside my spirit *did*, because as those words were coming out of my mouth, tears were sliding uncontrollably down my cheeks.

"Why am I crying?" I wondered. "This is really weird."

"THERE!" Susie exclaimed happily. "Now don't you feel better?"

I have no memory of what happened next, but many years later Susie told me I looked straight into her eyes as we sat on her bed and said, "Susie, I have this bad feeling that now I am going to have to face Satan!"

And *face Satan*, I did.

It wasn't long after I said that "sinners' prayer" when the scary thing in the house seemed to wake up. Terrifying things happened, mostly to me. One particular attack was something I called, "the hold me down thing!"

When I was lying on my bed—sometimes asleep and other times wide awake—an invisible force would come upon me and hold me down. I would literally be paralyzed! I was wide awake, and yet I was completely unable to move any part of my body.

I remember feeling the presence of evil when that happened. It was clearly demonic. But one time I was successful in tricking it.

I was paralyzed by the force and could not move, so instead of fighting and struggling to get up—which only caused the evil force to press down on me more tightly—I relaxed my body and pretended to go to sleep. Once I was fully relaxed, I waited about ten seconds and suddenly jumped up off my bed.

As soon as I started to move, I felt the spirit try to grab me and push me down again, but I had gotten a head start and was able to push through it. I then ran downstairs to tell my mom and dad what happened to me.

MY FIRST BAG OF METH

Growing up in Orange County, California, there was a strong cultural emphasis on physical appearance and status. Hollywood; beautiful, stick-thin, tanned models; and trendy couture were *in*, and chunky girls who loved to eat (that was me) were not. I longed for true happiness, identity, and purpose but had no clue where to find it.

So I went looking for it.

I was only nineteen when I hit the night club culture of money, cocaine, fast cars, and free-flowing alcohol. I got a job at a tanning salon and worked hard at becoming "beautiful." I was very tanned and started bleaching my hair. And in a desperate effort to achieve a model-thin frame, I drove to a seedy biker bar in Huntington Beach and met a woman who, I was told, had the answer to my weight problem.

She sold me a small bag of methamphetamine.

"This is the real deal," she convincingly explained. "If you want to lose weight, this is how to do it. But you must be very careful. This is very strong. It's called Peanut Butter Crank."

"I like peanut butter! What exactly do I do with this? How do I use it?" I asked as I held the small, clear baggie up in the women's restroom where we were completing the transaction.

I was so excited to try that crystal methamphetamine! I just knew it held the answer to my struggle with weight.

Her eyes grew wide as she exclaimed, "Oh, no! You've never done drugs! I shouldn't be selling this to you."

"No, please! I just need to lose twenty pounds! That's all I'm doing with this. Please tell me how to use it. Please!"

My pleading convinced the woman to sell me the meth and show me how to use it! I took it home and snorted my very first line the following morning.

It was the worst mistake of my life.

Within just a few years, a death grip of sin and addiction wound its way tightly around my throat, and I went down a dark road that took me on a journey straight to hell on earth. I was running a hundred miles an hour in the wrong direction, searching for love, peace, and purpose. And I believed the ultimate purpose in life was to attain happiness as it was defined by society.

I was wrong.

I was married at the age of twenty-one and divorced at twenty-two. What followed next was a string of abusive relationships as I dove headfirst into the dangerously toxic cycle of domestic violence. Some of the abuse was so disgusting and horrific that I can't—and won't ever—put it into words.

My self-esteem became nonexistent. On one hand, I was angry and hurt and believed I deserved better. On the other hand, I kept migrating toward men who were controlling and abusive. I used to tell myself that if I were loving enough, pretty enough, and thin enough, the abuse would stop, and my abusers would change. But what I didn't realize was their behavior was not about me at all.

All I knew was that nobody loved me for who I was. I believed the lie that I was not worthy of love. I believed the lies I was being told by man after man—that I was stupid, worthless, fat, and a piece of garbage. I was depressed. *Julie* was lost, and I had no idea how to get her back.

My parents encouraged me to return home, but they didn't know how to fix all that had been broken in my soul. I had become someone I never dreamed I would or could ever become. So when I was home, I was a full-blown alcoholic and meth-head sneaking into my parents' bedroom while they were asleep and stealing fifty-dollar bills from my dad's wallet.

I was a liar and a thief who would do anything to get more drugs, including sleeping with the dealer while convincing myself I was a girlfriend instead of a whore. It makes me weep now to write these words—to tell of my selfish, pathetic depravity.

But I *have* to tell you how deep my pit was and describe some of the steps that led me down to the very bottom so you will be able to comprehend the magnitude of my miraculous rescue and redemption.

As my addiction grew worse, so did a medical condition that began when I was eighteen. I started developing chronic pressure ulcers on the bottom of my left foot then, and by the time I divorced my first husband and moved back in with my parents, I had already had several surgeries trying to close and repair a large, chronic, badly infected foot ulcer.

The intravenous antibiotics I was receiving couldn't do their job in the presence of the increasing amount of alcohol and drugs coursing through my bloodstream.

Methamphetamine was no longer about weight loss; it was part of my daily life. I was hooked, but like most addicts, I was also in complete denial. I believed my alcohol and drug abuse was a choice instead of a dependency. I convinced myself that I made the choice to use because using made life more bearable.

I grew up watching my dear parents come home from work and have a couple of drinks every night "to wind down and take the edge off." So I thought consuming alcohol was a normal part of life, something to bring enjoyment and relaxation, and sometimes relief. What I didn't discover until I was an adult was that both of my grandfathers were alcoholics, and alcoholism ran rampant on both sides of my family—causing great pain and dysfunction that was passed down from generation to generation.

And then there was me!

THE VISION IN MY BEDROOM

A couple of years after my divorce and subsequent move back into my parents' house, I began to sense the presence of God again. One day I was upstairs in the middle bedroom of my parent's house. I remember leaning over a large wooden desk, cutting up a line of meth, and getting ready to snort it. Next to me was a glass tumbler containing Vodka and 7UP.

Suddenly, the ceiling above me and to the right opened up and disappeared. I looked up and saw a vision. A REAL vision! I saw myself in an orange prison jumpsuit standing behind a razor-wire fence.

I was in prison, but strangely, there was a smile on my face.

I wasn't upset or crying in the vision. Aside from the fact that I was in a prison jumpsuit on the wrong side of the razor-wire coils, I looked whole, healthy, happy, and at peace. And in that moment during the vision, I received what I know now was a word of knowledge—a *knowing.*

That *knowing* from God was that if I kept heading down the road I was going, I would end up in prison. But I also understood through that vision that I would one day change. I knew there would come a day when I would be sober, happy, and free—a day when I would turn into the *Julie* I longed so desperately to become.

But at the same time, I received yet another *knowing*—that by the time I finally turned my life around, neither of my parents would be alive to see it.

I was not a "Christian" when I experienced that vision, nor was I trying to be. And it was right there in my pathetic, strung-out, depraved state where God saw ME! But even more unbelievable, He WANTED me!

I knew in the middle of that moment that somehow God was longing to reach me. In the middle of my mess, the Holy Spirit was pursuing me with His great love and hope.

I looked back down at the white powdery line of methamphetamine neatly laid out and ready to snort. My eyebrows furrowed, and I felt a profound sadness deep within me that I couldn't explain. It felt like the very core of *Julie* was trapped someplace inside, longing to get out, to be free, to be a good girl, to be a success in life, to be loved, and to feel joy.

Looking back on that scene now, it makes me ponder in sadness, "Where had Julie gone? Where was that brown-haired little girl who loved getting ice cream cones with her dad at the drug store on Sunday afternoons and having Christmas Eve conversations with her little sister as they tried to stay awake long enough to catch Santa Claus eating the marshmallow fudge cookies?"

I left the bedroom and started to walk down the hallway when the Lord spoke to me (not out loud, but very clearly in my head). He said, "Julie, you can't have one foot in the world and one foot in my kingdom."

At that time, I was not even trying to live for, or seek, the Lord. I didn't even have *one foot* following Him. Yet in my fuzzy, clouded, desperate mind, I was able to figure out that the God who created me (yes, I believed that, even though I was deeply entrenched in sin) was trying to reach me and draw me into life—a life with Him.

I also understood that God was telling me I could not be double minded. I could not live for pleasure and do whatever I wanted to do and still become the woman He created me to become or live the life He created for me to live.

God was telling me the life I longed so desperately to live—a life full of peace, joy, family, relationships, career, love, and success—would be a byproduct of living single-mindedly and wholeheartedly for Him. And God was telling me in that single sentence that I was not going to experience that life *unless* I went *all-in* for Him and turned forever from my life of alcoholism, drug addiction, stealing, lying, and hurting everyone who loved me.

There was a war going on for my soul. And I had to choose which side I was going to be on.

Chapter 3

RUNNING AWAY FROM LIFE

DEEP INSIDE, MY dream was always to find a perfect husband. (Of course there are none). And I wanted to be the perfect wife. (There aren't any of those either). I dreamed of living in a cute house with a white picket fence—you know, like the ones you see in Hallmark movies.

In those movies, the woman heroine is always gorgeous with beautiful clothes and money to travel the world. In the end she marries a great guy who sweeps her off her feet, loves her deeply, and provides the perfect life. And they live together happily ever after.

That is not my story.

I was twenty-eight years old when gangrene set into my left foot. My temperature shot up to 106.5, and I woke up in the emergency room packed in ice from the neck down.

Hours later, I lay on a cold metal operating table gazing with trepidation at the circular saw suspended on the end of a surgical arm three feet above me. A nurse came in and put a tourniquet on my leg, tightening it so I would not bleed out during the operation.

The surgical team then came into the room, and another nurse started an IV. They didn't speak to me, comfort me, encourage me, or tell me that I was making the right choice by having my badly infected, gangrene-infested left leg amputated.

They knew I was an addict. When I looked into their eyes I could tell they viewed me as worthless trash.

There was only one person in the room who had a soft heart toward me—who believed my life was worth saving. That person was the orthopedic surgeon, the man in charge!

When I called his office crying four weeks earlier and told his secretary I was sick and had no medical insurance, that kind doctor agreed to see me. He saw how infected my limb was, and he knew the gaping, blackened, open wound at the tip of the remaining half of my foot (my toes had already been amputated) would kill me if it were not removed.

I later learned the medical team was in disbelief that the renowned orthopedic surgeon, who specialized in sports medicine, was performing the surgery at no cost to me—to save my life.

When I woke up in ICU after the amputation of my leg, my fever was gone. I could think clearly for the first time in over a decade.

It was truly miraculous!

The medical team had to give me five units of blood during the operation in order to save my life. I required fresh, uninfected, healthy blood in order to survive the ordeal.

The infected limb was cut off.

I was going to live!

My left leg was amputated below the knee. In time, I was fitted with a prosthesis, and I eventually learned to get around on it pretty well.

I was married to my second husband at the time, and we had a son—my only child. We named him Tyler. Tyler was one and a half years old when my leg was amputated. I was still struggling on and off with alcohol and drugs, and it was still a losing battle. My marriage was falling apart.

My second husband and I met in a bar and used together. But he got sober, while I remained trapped in the death grip of addiction. I lied to everyone about my addiction, and yet everyone knew something was very wrong with me.

In the midst of my struggle I didn't know where to turn for help. I felt desperate, hopeless, lost, deceitful, scared, and alone. The drugs and alcohol had so clouded my mind that I was unable to make good, sound decisions. Instead of going to rehab (which would have been an amazing idea) I left my husband, took Tyler, and moved across country to Tennessee.

I wanted to start life all over again. But in my frantic attempt to escape from all of my problems, I was not able to see that "I" was the biggest problem of all.

Somewhere deep inside of me I knew God was my answer, but I didn't know how to find Him. I was desperate for change, so I found a little Baptist church in the little rural town in Tennessee where we lived and went to church there one Sunday morning. I was desperate to become a new woman!

After the service, I gathered the courage to talk to the pastor and tell him I wanted to be baptized. I thought that was my answer. Surely I would come up out of the water in the baptismal tank a brand-new woman. I was going to become the beautiful Hallmark mom I had always longed so desperately to become.

The following Sunday morning during service, the pastor announced that the new lady in town wanted to be baptized, and he called me up front. I already had a white baptismal robe on over my clothing, and I stepped into the tank with him. It was *my big moment*!

The pastor put his hands on my head and said, "Julie, because you have repented of your sins, I now baptize you in the name of the Father and the Son and the Holy Spirit."

As I was going under the water, all I could think was,

"Repent of my sins? What's THAT?"

That pastor never spoke to me about my reasons for wanting to be baptized. He never told me I was a sinner—or what sin even was! I had no real understanding of what I was doing, so instead of coming up out of the water a changed woman, I came up out of the water a soaking wet woman.

I was unchanged and didn't have a clue how to live for God. And I had no idea there was such a thing as a real, living relationship with Jesus Christ.

Further, nobody at that little church took me under wing and tried to disciple me. Nobody asked me if I had a Bible and read it every day. No one even asked if I knew how to pray. Every Sunday for a month following my baptism, I walked out of that little country church and stood in the gravel parking lot, holding my little two-year-old Tyler in my arms. I wanted so desperately for someone—*anyone*—to invite me out to lunch and befriend me.

No one ever did. I was depressed and lonelier than ever.

THE DAY MY SON WAS TAKEN

Tyler's dad found me two years later, and an ugly, vicious custody battle began. I was thirty-three years old and felt like I was losing my mind. My already dysfunctional life began to unravel at the seams. My greatest fear was that I would lose my little boy—my precious, delightful, funny little Tyler—and it was starting to happen.

I knew I was living on the edge. I knew my life of alcohol, meth, pills, and carousing wasn't acceptable.

Oh, how I *longed* to be a good mother! In my heart I had a vision of the perfect mom baking cookies and grilling burgers while all the neighborhood kids came to my house to play with Tyler. But I had no idea how to get from the despicable woman I was to the momma I desperately longed to become.

Every night when I put Tyler to bed, he begged me, "Momma! Read me a bedtime story."

That was one of my favorite parts of the day—perhaps because reading my baby his bedtime stories was really what I felt a good mother should do. But I loved reading to Tyler. Each time I finished a story, he cried out with delight, "Momma! One more. One more story!"

After a few stories I always admonished him with, "This is the last story, Tyler. Say it with me." Then Tyler smiled up at me and exclaimed, "LAST story! This is the last story, Momma."

As I tucked him in and kissed him good night, he always locked his little arms around my neck and hung on for dear life. I had to pry his arms loose and tell him to go to sleep.

During that custody battle, I must have walked down the hallway of our rented home to Tyler's bedroom ten times every night to look at him. I cracked open his door wider and stood in the doorway watching my beloved four-year-old sleeping peacefully.

Deep inside, I knew I was going to lose him because of my life choices and the mess I had created. But even the sharp pain I felt in my heart over that couldn't stop me from going down my path of destruction. No matter how miserable I was, no matter how much I hated myself, I just couldn't seem to stop.

At one point in the custody battle it became more evident than ever that I was about to have Tyler taken away from me. And even though I wanted so desperately to do the right thing for my precious little boy, in a frantic attempt to run away from all my problems—*again*—I took my beloved four-year-old Tyler and fled to Mexico to hide.

But after ten days in Mexico, the realization that I needed to try to work things out struck me hard, and I decided to return home.

As I was crossing back into the United States, I was taken into Secondary Inspection by a border protection officer. Tyler didn't know what was happening. We were there all day. Finally, at 8:00 PM the officers put Tyler in one police car and me in another.

There I was, handcuffed for the first time in my life. As we drove off down the 5 Freeway, I suddenly heard Tyler's sweet little voice over the police radio, "Hi, Momma. I love you, Momma!"

I knew that was the moment I had been dreading.

Deep down inside, I knew that day was coming, and as I heard Tyler's happy voice over the radio, I knew he had no idea that he might never see me again. The detective driving me leaned forward, picked up her hand-held radio, and held it up to the cage separating the front and back seats.

With the weight of my sins crushing my chest, all I could think of in that moment was that I didn't want my son to be afraid.

The sun was setting in the city of San Diego, and all the city lights were coming on. If it were not for the fact that for the first time in my life I was handcuffed and sitting in the back of a police car, it would have been a beautiful ride. I leaned forward to get as close to the radio as I could, and I answered Tyler with forced excitement in my voice.

"Tyler! look at all those beautiful lights, Tyler! Do you see them?"

Tyler's joyful little voice came right back over the radio, "Oh yeaaah, Momma! Those lights are beauuuutiful, Momma! I love you, Momma!"

"I love you, Tyler! Momma loves you SO MUCH."

My heart was ripped completely out of my chest that day.

ONE BAD DECISION AFTER ANOTHER

I was in an Orange County jail for three weeks for misdemeanor child stealing. When I was released, I was assigned to a probation officer to whom I was required to report on a regular basis. I returned to my parents' house and discovered I had a six-month restraining order against me that prevented me from contacting either my ex-husband or my son.

I called an attorney who was a friend of my parents, and I explained the whole situation to him including my panicked run to Mexico with Tyler. When I asked him if there was any way he or any other attorney could help me get even supervised visits with my son, he told me in no uncertain terms that I had made a fatal error.

"The best thing you can do is just wait until your son turns eighteen and then try to find him," he explained regretfully. "You really blew it, Julie. No attorney in his right mind would be willing to help you now. You need to focus on getting your life together."

After that conversation I walked out to my parent's backyard and sat down on the deck overlooking the beautiful, sparkling pool. I grew up in that house. That was the yard I played in as a little girl, chasing Myrtle, our desert tortoise, around with grapes and lettuce.

I began seriously reflecting on things.

"How did everything go so wrong?" I asked myself.

"How did it all come to this?"

"It has to be me. It's . . . ME!

My dad walked out and sat down beside me. He loved me so much, but he didn't know how to fix me. Tears rolled slowly down my cheeks. Without lifting my head to look at him, I said, "Dad, I hurt everyone I love. Everyone who gets close to me gets destroyed. I ruin everything."

"That's not true!" my dad insisted through his own tears.

I was starting to see that I was the problem and the cause of everything that had happened to me. I was beginning to understand that my life was a mess and how I somehow had caused so much pain to so many people.

My dad didn't know what to say or how to help me. While he was not blind to everything I had done, he had no idea what it would take to end my pain and change my life. All he knew was that his little girl was hurting, so he was hurting too.

That afternoon when my parents were taking a nap, I wrote a note telling them I was leaving. Consumed with guilt, shame, and depression, I told my mom and dad that I didn't want to cause them any more pain or be any further trouble to them. I then laid the pen down slowly on the white tile kitchen counter next to the note.

I barely remember taking a taxi to the Greyhound bus station and heading—once again—to the Mexican border.

Oh, how I longed for an end to the craziness. How I would have given anything for somebody to stop me. I was on a self-destructive path, and for some weird reason, I just couldn't seem to stop myself. One bad decision led to a worse decision, and my life just kept gaining downhill momentum.

DAD NEVER MADE IT OUT OF THE HOSPITAL

Once in Mexico, I headed back to the same little studio apartment in which I had stayed with Tyler for ten days during my panicked run during the custody battle. The apartment in Tijuana was one block from the ocean, and the very nice Mexican apartment manager, Jose, had put my clothes in a bag and kept them for me. I decided it was as good a place as any to stay for a while.

Maybe I could clear my head. Maybe I could even start a new life. But everywhere I looked, I thought of Tyler—*my baby*! The pain was unbearable, so I went to the store and came back with beer, rum, and coke—as much as I could carry. I made a cold drink, and then another, and another, until I finally staggered to the bathroom, washed my face, put on my pajamas, and passed out on the bed.

After a couple of days I decided to try to do something that would feel normal, something I loved to do more than anything. I grew up loving the ocean, so I put on my bikini, grabbed a towel and tanning oil, made a stiff drink, and headed to the beach known as Playas de Tijuana. I climbed down a steep cliff to get to an abandoned strip of sand, spread out my towel, and lay down.

The warmth of the sun penetrated my body, and I tried to force myself to focus on that warmth without any thoughts. No thinking! Thinking hurt—Bad!

I was watching seagulls flying back and forth like the restless kites of children when, after an hour, I turned my head and saw two men in the distance walking toward me. The beach was otherwise empty, so I thought it was odd. I shielded my eyes from the sun and kept watching the men as they drew closer and closer.

One of the men was very tall, with silvery white hair. And as he drew closer I could see he wore a smile as wide as the ocean itself. He was with a short Mexican man. Something about that tall man was familiar, and I couldn't take my eyes off of him. Then, as they continued to walk toward me, I sat straight up.

It was my DAD!

My dad was walking toward me on an empty beach in a foreign country where I had not told him I was going. He knew I was a mess. He knew I was lost and broken. And he loved me so much that he went looking for me.

He was so desperate to find me that he searched apartments in the city of Tijuana until he found the one where I was staying. The kind apartment manager, who had seen me heading to the beach with a towel, told him where I went; but finding me was not that simple. To get to that deserted beach, I had to walk to the edge of a large cliff and climb down a very steep, dangerous hill covered with jagged rocks. And in order to get to me, my dad had to descend down the same way.

His act of love was nothing short of a miracle to me. And that miracle proved to be even more amazing when I later discovered that my dad was dying of lung cancer at the time.

I scrambled to my feet with a huge smile and shouted, "DAD! How did you find me?"

Dad explained how he and my mom searched Tijuana until they found my apartment. We hugged each other tightly, and together we climbed back up the jagged hill to my mom, who was waiting at the top. The three of us walked back to my dingy apartment, and they inquired, "Well, Julie, what are you going to do now? Are you just going to live here forever in this room?"

That was exactly what I planned to do—live in that seedy, shady little room and stay numb, forever. In my deranged thinking, Mexico was a safe place. And I didn't have to think about a job, because my Social Security Disability checks that I began receiving after the amputation of my leg were sufficient to live on.

Eventually, though, my parents convinced me to return home with them. I decided that I would be closer to Tyler when the restraining order ended, and I could attempt to see him. But when I tried to call to talk to him six months later, I found the phone had been disconnected. I was heartbroken. The thought of never seeing my son again was almost unbearable.

Then, on Christmas Eve that same year, my Dad went to get an x-ray because he was having some chest pain. The news came back quickly. Dad had stage-four lung cancer.

He was scheduled to have surgery and have the bottom third of his right lung removed, and after that, he was supposed to be fine. My mom and I drove him to Fountain Valley Hospital on the morning of January 4, 1998.

Right after the surgery, the doctor came to the waiting room to tell us that the cancer was worse than he thought. It had spread to the chambers surrounding his heart.

My tall, handsome, brilliant, loving, funny dad never made it out of the hospital.

On the twenty-first of January, he was gone.

THE FASTEST ONE-LEGGED RUNNER

The day of my dad's funeral fell on the first day I was to check in with my probation officer. When I called to tell her in tears about me losing my dad—brokenly explaining that my dad had just died of lung cancer and that I could not keep my appointment the following week because of the funeral—she sarcastically replied,

"I have heard that story before, hundreds of times. Your dad did NOT die. I am NOT an idiot."

At that moment it was like a light switch shut off in my head. I gave up on life. I had no coping skills to deal with death. All I knew how to do was numb pain with substances. Any thread of desire to try to navigate my way successfully through probation—or life—vanished. I no longer cared whether I lived or died.

My son was gone.

My dad was dead.

Somehow, in a mental fog, I made it through the funeral, and then I did what I did best of all.

I prepared to leave.

I didn't think about my grieving mother or consider the fact that I would be leaving her all alone to deal with the untimely death of her husband of almost forty years. Nor did I think about the potential legal consequences of my decision. My mind was fuzzy from years of meth addiction. And with the unbearable loss of my dad, I went into panic-mode.

Once again I did what was becoming my trademark response to tough times.

I ran—back to Mexico.

I was the fastest one-legged runner I knew.

The only problem was that everywhere I went, there I was. And I was my biggest problem!

I had thoughts of ending my life many times a day. And I had only been in Mexico for a few days when someone told me I could go to a pharmacist, hand him a twenty-dollar bill, and receive bottles of narcotics.

"That's my answer!" I thought.

"I'll just take a handful of pills and never wake up again. It'll be easy—painless."

"I'll DO it!"

A couple of hours and one shady medical visit later, I returned to the seedy little studio apartment I had rented and dumped a large pile of narcotics on the dresser.

Staring at the pills, I thought about how up to that point I had done nothing but mess up my life. I destroyed everything. I couldn't succeed at anything. But then I began to reason that if I swallowed those pills, I just might wake up again and have to face a horrible aftermath of being in a semi-vegetative state, or something even worse. With my luck, I would very likely fail even at suicide. I would probably only make another mess of things.

So I devised a different plan, and with a swift swoop of my hand, I pushed the pills into the top dresser drawer and shut it. I decided to take a couple of pills each day, along with margaritas or whatever alcohol I happened to be drinking that day, and I would just keep myself high and numb.

But that didn't help either, and things for me just continued to go from bad to worse.

First Corinthians 15:33 says, *"Don't be fooled by those who say such things, for 'bad company corrupts good character.'"*

I found this to be incredibly true. I eventually ended up running into some fellow Americans who were living in Baja California, Mexico. We were like magnets drawn to one another, and they were *bad company*.

Now, I must make it clear that my character was definitely NOT what anyone would call good at that time, but the people I met and befriended took my character to a whole new level. They were mafia, with huge drug cartel associations in several countries.

They were cooking huge quantities of crystal methamphetamine in their home. I'm not talking about bathtub crank or small amounts of meth. I'm talking about big glass flasks, dangerous chemicals, huge tubing, billowing smoke, and near-death accidents when the house should have blown up because the meth cooks fell asleep during the cooking process.

For me, running away from life never changed things for the better; I had already lost everything else, and I was well on the way to losing my mind.

Chapter 4

GOD LOVES BROKEN THINGS

AT FIRST I was afraid to befriend those people who were involved in drug manufacturing and distribution. I heard about how the Mexican Drug Task Force, known as the Mexican Federales, raided one of their previous homes by jumping over the fence wearing black masks with machine guns in hand. But I was still drawn to them, and mostly it was because they had two little boys close to my Tyler's age.

I felt sorry for those boys living under those circumstances, and I spent time taking them to the beach or making them food to eat. That soothed my loneliness since I was missing Tyler so desperately. And it helped open my eyes to how incredibly irresponsible it is to expose children to a home with alcohol, drugs, drug deals, partying, and the dangers that invariably go hand in hand with all of it.

One morning I took the boys for a walk on the beach. We played a game to see who could pick up the most shells. There were shells and sand dollars littering the sand, and I was becoming an avid collector during long, thoughtful morning walks on the Mexico beaches.

Suddenly, both boys saw a giant shell. They ran to grab it at the same time, but Sam, being a little bigger, got there first and scooped it up. Dylan was crestfallen as he walked slowly over to me and opened his hand to show me that all he had was one jagged, broken seashell.

A strange and powerful feeling engulfed me in that moment, and I suddenly felt this unexplainable love and presence with us. I started to explain to Dylan that God loves broken things. I told Dylan that broken things are very special to God, and because of that, he had the best shell of all.

I had no idea at the time where that idea came from or how I knew it, but somehow I knew the words coming out of my mouth were actually true. That caused me to begin feeling a sense of awe and wonder as I stood on the sandy beach with two little boys who were not even mine and pondered my own life and the *absolute brokenness* that was *me*.

I had no idea at the time that God's Word declares, *"He heals the brokenhearted and bandages their wounds"* (Psalm 147:3). And I had no idea that God's Word says, *"We can make our plans, but the Lord determines our steps"* (Proverbs 16:9).

Verse twelve of Hebrews chapter four tells us the Word of God is *"sharper than the sharpest two-edged sword, cutting between soul and spirit, between joint and marrow. It exposes our innermost thoughts and desires."*

The Word of God does what it says it will do—without fail, and without compromise.

God's Word is holy, precious, and true! And when it is prayed and decreed over a person, it reaches inside of the soul, creates an awareness of the absence of God, and creates a hunger for Him. And that can ultimately alter the course of the life over which it is spoken. I know now that someone was praying God's Word over me, and those fervent prayers were causing something to stir within me.

As I stood on that sandy beach, a vivid memory flashed through my mind of a woman I met at a bank in Tennessee when I still had Tyler and was running away from life. I had run to a little southern town where I knew no one. But even in that town I was a magnet for the wrong people. In fact, I attracted them quickly.

I soon met a man who was a drug addict and a thief with a horrible reputation. He quickly stole a few hundred dollars from me, and that caused my rent check to bounce. Embarrassed, I went to the bank to talk to the teller and explain what happened.

As is common in small southern towns, the bank teller, whom I had previously not met, had already heard all about the wayward mother who moved to town with her little boy. She looked kindly into my eyes and said, "I am praying for you."

I glared at her and stated coldly, "I don't *need* your prayers! Do not pray for me!"

I could tell she was a bit taken aback by what I said and wasn't sure how to respond. Everything about that caring woman was humble and genuine. Something inside wanted to burst into tears, so I quickly turned my head so as to not see her gentle eyes. She then softly replied, "Okay."

I believe with all my heart that kind woman still prayed for me after that encounter in the bank. In fact, I believe my harsh response broke her heart and caused her to pray earnestly for my salvation.

I remember our conversation and her sweet face as if it were yesterday—even though I'm sitting here writing this book twenty-two years later. You see, besides praying for me, that woman planted a seed in my soul.

My sister, Susie, planted a seed within me years earlier when she held my hands and made me say a sinner's prayer with her when I was a young teenager. And that sweet woman in the bank gently planted another seed—a seed of faith that God was real, that He saw me in my brokenness, that He WANTED me, that He had a PLAN for me, and that He loves *broken things.*

THE RED LEATHER BIBLE

I have no idea where I got it, but somehow—there in Mexico—I had a Bible. It had a red leather cover, and it was one of those easy-to-read versions. I have a faint memory of grabbing that red Bible from my mom's house in my desperate rush to pack and flee to Mexico. It could have very well been my dad's Bible, but I'm not sure.

On many days, I took that Bible up to the terrace of the house I was renting and read it there. I had moved from the little seedy studio apartment to a beautiful two-story house. I rented the back part of the house from an older American woman who was living in the front. I could often be found lying outside in my bathing suit on that terrace with my Bible beside an ice-cold Corona with a slice of lime shoved inside the neck.

I was on a journey, and the Lord began to woo me, teach me, and speak to me during that crazy season of being a strung-out alcoholic fugitive on the run in Mexico.

There is no place you can go to hide from God.

I can never escape from your Spirit!
I can never get away from your presence!
If I go up to heaven, you are there;
if I go down to the grave, you are there.
If I ride the wings of the morning,
if I dwell by the farthest oceans,
even there your hand will guide me,
and your strength will support me.
I could ask the darkness to hide me
and the light around me to become night—
but even in darkness I cannot hide from you.
(Psalm 139: 7-12a)

I thought I was running away from life, but in reality, I ran to Mexico and met the Holy Spirit!

I opened up that red Bible and read verses that told me things like the righteous will inherit the kingdom of heaven, and the wicked will perish and burn. And an unfamiliar sense of conviction came over me as I read about what happens to those who turn away from God. After reading such things, I often quickly closed the Bible.

Somehow I knew I was "the wicked!" I knew it was talking about me.

I always believed in God, but when I was young my parents took me and my little sister to a Christian Science Church and Sunday school. I remember the teacher telling me that sickness and death were not real, and neither was Satan. I was only twelve years old at the time, but I had a Bible, and I read in it about sickness, death, and Satan.

Something deep inside of me knew what I read was right, and my Sunday school teacher was wrong. I told my dad I didn't want to go to that church anymore because the teacher lied to me. So at twelve, after attending that Christian Science Church for a few years, my dad, who didn't know how to respond to my revelation, stopped taking us to that church—or any other church.

Something in Mexico kept drawing me to that red Bible. And another unfamiliar thing began happening to me as well. Every time I drove by a church in Mexico that had a church sign saying *Iglesia Pentecostal*, my heart started beating faster, and something in my spirit quickened.

I had this *knowing* that there was something in that church for me. I had a powerful sense that something in that church would change my life. And when I drove past one of those churches, I often decided I was going to go there on the following Sunday.

But I was always high when Sunday came. I was never sober enough to walk into a church, so I never went.

THE BULLET THAT MISSED

A gun shot went off on New Year's Eve of the year 2000 while I was standing on the rooftop terrace of my rented two-story house in Playas de Tijuana. I felt the heat of the bullet as it passed within a fraction of an inch of my face.

I still remember the shockwave of terror that washed over me. I'm convinced that angels were there on assignment, surrounding me that night to save my life. To the rest of the world I was nothing more than another pathetic, strung out, addicted, desperate, drug-smuggling fugitive on the run who was hiding from the Mexican Drug Task Force and the United States Marshals.

But to Jesus, I know now that I was someone worth forgiving and dying for.

I realized instantly the bullet had just missed my face. Eyes wide with fear, I quickly dropped down and army-crawled across the Spanish tile terrace to the stairs. I tore down the stairs and locked myself inside the house.

"Who was that?" I wondered in shock, "Who shot at me? I don't think they meant to miss me. The bullet was too close. What in the world am I doing here in Mexico, anyway? I'm cut off from my entire family. What kind of life is this? I could die here, and nobody would even miss me for a long time."

What I didn't know yet, though, was that God had a divine mission for me, a special assignment that He had planned just for me from the beginning of time.

> *For we are God's masterpiece. He has created us anew in Christ Jesus, so we can do the good things he planned for us long ago.* (Ephesians 2:10)

Psalm 139 assures us that God himself knit us together in our mothers' wombs, And it tells us that all our days are ordained for us. I believe that included the day the angels cushioned my face from that bullet!

Even in my ugliest, most desperate, hopeless moment, God still had plans for my life. And they were *"plans for good and not for disaster, to give* [ME] *a future and a hope"* (Jeremiah 29:11b).

It was not in God's plan for me to take a bullet in Mexico, for it was not much longer before I came face to face with my Savior!

THE BAG LADY

I needed to leave Playas de Tijuana. The bullet was a sign that I was too close to the wrong people. So it was time to run again. I heard Rosarito Beach was not only beautiful and affordable but also had great tacos. (I love tacos!) So I packed my belongings into a cardboard box, got into a taxi, and headed south.

No matter how many years go by, there are a few events I will never forget. The bullet episode was one. Another happened shortly after I moved to Rosarito Beach.

I was walking down the street in Rosarito Beach while moving to a local hotel from a camper I had been staying in. I did that in another effort to run away from the wrong people and a life that was becoming more dangerous by the day.

I had no transportation, and with all my belongings packed into a single, large, heavy cardboard box, I was staggering underneath the weight of the box with sweat running down the sides of my forehead. I didn't even stop to think about what I must have looked like to a bystander.

Suddenly I heard the voice of a teenage boy behind me. In a loud, demeaning tone, he mocked, "Hey! Look at the bag lady!"

I turned to look over my shoulder. I couldn't imagine he was speaking about me.

But he WAS.

He was with two of his friends, and they were all dressed in expensive *adidas* gear. They obviously were from families with money. My box was growing heavier with each step. I felt deep shame and embarrassment wash over me.

I wanted to run and hide, but my box was too heavy. All I could do was continue to walk down the street and pretend I didn't hear them. But thoughts about what the boy shouted in derision rushed through my mind as I walked.

"This is what I've been reduced to. 'A Bag Lady!'" I thought. "They have no idea! They don't know my dad was an optometrist. And my mom is an electrical aerospace engineer. I grew up in a big house in a nice suburb of Southern California. I'm from a family with money too.

"I'm not a bag lady! I'm just a lady who happens to be walking down the street to a hotel with a cardboard box containing all of my belongings because I don't have a home or family."

"Wait—am I a bag lady? Maybe I am!"

"Is this how far I've fallen? What am I doing here anyway, alone, in a foreign country?"

Chapter 5

HOW DID IT ALL COME TO THIS?

I STAYED IN the hotel in Rosarito Beach until my next Social Security Disability check arrived, and then I rented and moved into a two bedroom house. I lived there in that house in Rosarito Beach for a couple of months until there was yet another attempt made on my life.

After that, I ran yet again and ended up farther south in Ensenada. The meth cooks I had associated with soon after I ran back into Mexico after my dad died had by that time also moved to Ensenada to stay a step ahead of the Federales, and I met them there.

My financial situation improved some during my stay in Ensenada, and while I continued being strung out with my life in a mess, I still had the wherewithal to secure an automobile and establish at least a semblance of stability even though it was not destined to last long.

THE FIRST TIME I HEARD THE VOICE IN MEXICO

I had been awake for seventy-two hours straight—and so high that I was waxing my Mustang inside my garage at three o'clock in the morning. By 9:30 am I realized I was out of both alcohol and money, so I scrounged around until I found a pocketful of change and headed to the liquor store to buy a forty ounce can of beer.

As I drove to the store on that bright, sunny morning, a voice spoke to me. It was not an audible voice, but as clear as it was to me, it may as well have been.

"Julie, you're going to hell for the way you're living."

It was simple and straightforward, just like that.

It wasn't an angry voice. It was just matter of fact. And it was so clear in my hearing that I answered back. I believed in both heaven and hell—just like I believed in God—but at that point in my life, heaven and hell seemed more like abstract concepts rather than reality.

"Well, at least I'm going to have fun while I'm going there!" I retorted aloud.

As soon as those words left my mouth, I realized that I was NOT actually having fun at all. There was a season in my life when the drinking, partying, carousing, and sinning had *seemed* like fun and *felt* like fun. But as my own words echoed in my head, I realized that the life I was living had not *been* fun for a long time.

Then I heard my own voice speak again—out loud.

"Well, I guess I'm not really having fun."

I didn't doubt for a moment that what I heard was the truth.

And I knew the voice was from God.

THE DAY THE BLINDERS CAME OFF

I tugged and tugged, but my shoe would not come off. It had been a long couple of days that I had been running on meth without any sleep, and I was ready to take a shower and go to bed. I knew that something was not right as I continued to tug on my tennis shoe.

Nervously, I undid the laces and loosened them. I tugged on my shoe again. Nothing. It wouldn't come off of my foot. I started to get a sick feeling in the pit of my stomach, and I slowly rotated my foot so I could see the bottom.

In shock, I discovered I had stepped on a rusty construction nail, and it had literally nailed my shoe to my foot. I was not aware of it, because in addition to my drugged condition, the chronic neuropathy that I had long dealt with robbed me of a normal sense of feeling in my foot.

Visions of the infected ulcers that had caused the amputation of my left leg flooded my mind. With much difficulty, I pulled out the nail. I had to pull hard to get it to come loose. I took my shoe and sock off dreading what I knew I was about to see, and there in the bottom of my foot was a hole about an inch deep and one-quarter inch wide—right where the nail had been.

I was horrified!

Within less than a week my foot swelled to the size of a small football, and there was a red streak running up my leg. The hole quickly transformed into a deep, gaping, infected ulcer the size of a silver dollar that was sending poison into my bloodstream, and I could see badly infected flesh and ligaments. In addition, the wound emitted a very foul odor.

Terrified, I went to see an American doctor who had a small practice in Mexico. He took one look at my foot, looked into my face with deep concern, and said, "You're in big trouble. You're probably going to lose this leg too."

The kind doctor tried his best to talk me into going back to the States to get good medical care. Without telling him I was a fugitive living on the run (having broken probation when I ran back to Mexico), I simply repeated over and over, "I can't go back. I can't go back."

I don't remember how I got home from that doctor's appointment. I just remember walking in the back door of my house overlooking the ocean. I staggered to the living room where I crumpled to the floor. Deep sobs shook my body as all the pain I had walked through for so many years came flooding to the surface.

I had been tormented by evil in the form of spirits, humans, and society. I had been betrayed by those who are supposed to nurture and protect. I had lost my leg. I had lost my beloved dad. I had lost my only child. And now, I was about to lose my only remaining leg and any bit of sanity I had left.

I was living as a fugitive in a foreign country, and I had no health insurance. I already had a fever from the infection in my foot, and without medical treatment I would surely die. But as I was about to lapse into a state of stunned and helpless desperation, I felt the presence of God enter the living room as though God himself were hovering above me, close to the ceiling.

It was HIM!

In a supernatural, God-ordained moment, the Holy Spirit descended from heaven and pulled the blinders off my eyes that had been there for so many years.

You see, for all those years I thought of myself as a victim. Poor me, I was born with spina bifida. Poor me, I was one of those disabled people. Poor me, I went through a string of abusive men. Poor me, I lost my son. Poor me, my dad was dead, and the list went on and on.

I always had an excuse for drinking and doing drugs and walking through life anesthetized. Up to that moment I had never taken any responsibility for the mess I had made of my life nor for the hurt I had caused to those I loved. But in that moment my life flashed before my eyes, and I finally understood—for the first time ever—that *I was a sinner in need of a Savior.*

I was finally overcome with grief over the person I had become.

The wailing within me grew louder. And from the depth of my being I began to cry out to God. For the first time in my life I understood, beyond a shadow of a doubt, that I needed Him, and He alone could save me.

"God!" I cried to Him, "I don't know if you can hear me. And I don't know how to pray. And I don't know if you're listening. But if you are, Lord, I'm in a world of evil so deep that if I keep going I will never make it back to reality or sanity.

"God, I need you. I need you! God! I NEED You!"

"God, I've been trying to quit drinking and quit using drugs, but I CAN'T! I keep writing in my journal that I won't drink or use drugs anymore starting Monday. But Monday never comes. God, I can't meet you halfway. I need you to DO IT ALL!

"God, help me! Do whatever it takes. I need you to become the very center of my life or I'll be lost forever!"

I wailed and sobbed and cried out to God for what seemed like an eternity. Then, when the sobbing subsided, I got up from my knees, made a stiff drink, and passed out.

That was how I went to bed every night. I didn't go to sleep. I drank until I passed out.

CROSSING THE BORDER

I pulled myself out of bed the next morning and stumbled to the kitchen to boil some water and make a big cup of coffee. The ocean churned, and a morning mist hung low over the white capped waves that crashed restlessly on the shore.

I didn't feel any different. I had cried out to God with everything I had the previous night, but that morning I felt the same as the day before. I was emotionally spent, spiritually anguished, raw, and empty. My dad was still dead. Tyler was still gone. I was still a fugitive. My foot still had a huge, infected hole in the bottom of it, and nothing seemed any different.

What I didn't yet understand, though, was that since I cried out to the God of the universe and gave Him permission to take over (literally inviting Him into the center of my life), He was already at work behind the scenes. He was already orchestrating events to turn my life—a life that I felt was meaningless—into a life of purpose.

There was a knock at the back door, and in came my friends, the meth cooks. They arrived to ask me if I would take a large amount of drugs across the border for money that day. A strange sort of haze clouded my mind. I didn't care if I lived or died, so I didn't see any reason not to do it.

I stood silently in the living room as they carried in the drugs and fastened the four pounds of crystal methamphetamine around my waist. The meth was in gallon-size plastic bags pressed almost flat and covered by five thick, tight layers of silver duct tape.

If I were the author of my story moving forward, I definitely would have penned it differently. But when I cried out to God the night before and gave Him full permission to do whatever it took to become the center of my life, I handed Him the pen!

I had surrendered authorship of my life to the One who created it in the first place. And even though it already looked like all was lost, things seemed to get even worse when that series of steel prison doors slammed shut behind me as I was ushered into the Metropolitan Correctional Center in San Diego before the sun went down.

MOM, I'M IN PRISON!

I didn't want to call my mom from the inmate telephone hanging on the wall. I knew if she answered her phone and heard the recording of "This is a call from a federal prison," it might cause her already weakened heart to stop beating altogether.

I approached the lieutenant at the correctional center, and with desperation in my voice, I convinced him to let me use his desk phone after I described my mother's condition. She had recently undergone open-heart surgery to receive her mechanical mitral valve, and that was followed by a stroke that occurred immediately after waking up from the anesthesia.

With hot tears of grief and guilt flowing down my face, I told him how my dad, her best friend, had died unexpectedly from lung cancer just two years earlier, and I assured him that my mom, still grieving her loss, might have a heart attack if she answered her phone and heard that dreadful recording.

My hands were shaking as I dialed the familiar number. Then Mom answered with, "Hello?"

My mom's unsuspecting voice came through the phone and stabbed me in the heart. She had no idea!

What I *wanted* to say was, "Mom, I did something wrong. I was arrested with drugs, Mom. I've been struggling with drugs for years and haven't been honest about it. I'm a liar! I'm a thief! I need help. I'm desperate! I'm tired of my life being a mess. I'm glad I got arrested. I'm tired of running."

Instead, what I said was, "Hi Mom, how are you?"

The lieutenant gave me the look. I knew I had to make it brief and to the point.

"Mom, I have to tell you something, and you're going to get upset, but I don't want you to worry about me. I'm calling to tell you that I was arrested, and I'm in prison."

Immediately my mother exclaimed, "No you're not! You aren't in prison, Honey. You didn't do anything!"

"I know."

"Yikes! Was that really me? Did I really just say, 'I know'—as in, I did nothing wrong?" I thought to myself.

"Mom, I have to go now, but I'll call you again. Please don't worry about me. Everything is going to be okay."

One week later, wearing a wrinkled khaki jumpsuit, I stood handcuffed and shackled in front of a United States federal judge.

My mother was in the courtroom, her face blotchy from days of crying.

It was surreal when my case was announced in open court: *The United States of America versus Julie DeVere Fitzpatrick.*

Our eyes met as the judge slammed his gavel down on the majestic wooden podium. I was arraigned at *seventeen years to life.* The sadness in my mom's eyes broke my heart. I wanted to crawl under a rock. My face was flushed with shame.

I would have given anything to have been able to run out of the courtroom that day. The agony I had caused my mom was etched on her face, and I couldn't undo it.

Chapter 6

THE MOMENT THAT CHANGED EVERYTHING

THE REALITY OF being in federal prison hit me in the gut like a ton of bricks. The fact I had ended up there was unfathomable. Many of the female inmates were from Mexico. And most of the crimes the inmates committed were United States border crimes involving either drugs or human trafficking.

I heard the term "drug mule," and I was informed that I was one of them.

I was not in an actual cell. Instead, I was on the sixth floor of the Metropolitan Correctional Center in a wide-open dorm containing groupings of metal bunk beds. There were four bunk beds (eight women) in each cluster.

I sat alone, cross-legged on my bunk while the others were off playing cards or watching television. I had received a Bible from the chaplain and was trying to read it, but waves of depression and despair kept sweeping over me as finally the reality of losing Tyler—that reality I had worked so hard to numb for so long—began to sink in.

The pain in my heart was almost unbearable. Unable to stop the surge of hot tears sliding down my face, I glanced up in time to see a small group of well-dressed, manicured women walk into our pod. One of them looked straight at me. Our eyes met, and without hesitation, she marched straight over to my bunk bed and sat down next to me.

"Do you know that Jesus loves you very much?" she asked.

"Not me," I mumbled, as my tears turned into a downpour. "I've done too many things wrong. I've gone too far and been too evil for God to forgive me!"

But that didn't seem to faze the kind, godly woman, and she patiently continued to insist it didn't matter what I had done. She explained that Jesus Christ hung and died on a cross to forgive me of my sins—every last one of them. She persisted in assuring me that nothing I had done was beyond God's grace or His willingness and ability to forgive me.

As she spoke earnestly and with conviction, I knew it was the truth, and I felt an unfamiliar HOPE begin to rise in my heart. I suddenly remembered the prayer that I had said with Susie, and at last I understood its meaning.

That evening when all the other inmates were off eating dinner, I stayed behind and knelt down beside my bunk on that cold, hard cement floor. Through deep, painful, and broken sobs, I begged Jesus to forgive me for every sin I had ever committed, and I asked Him to be my Lord and Savior.

"Jesus, I've messed everything up so badly!" I wailed. "I don't see how you could possibly fix the mess I've made, but if anyone can, I believe it's you! I'm thirty-five years old, and I've completely destroyed my life. I'm sorry, Jesus. I'm SO SORRY. My life is yours now, Jesus! What can you do with it? Do whatever you want to with it!"

"I'm done! I SURRENDER!"

As I prayed, I sensed Jesus was very close to me. His presence and His love were tangible.

Mysteriously, none of the women returned from dinner until after my intimate, noisy prayer session ended. I arose from the cement floor a *saved woman*. Forgiven! Set free!

I slept like a rock that night.

I was moved to a different cluster in the pod the very next day. And three of the women there were holding a daily Bible study. They asked me if I wanted to join them. Ecstatic, I accepted immediately.

HOPE REPLACES HOPELESSNESS

A bit of humor seeped in from time to time and lessened the severity of my circumstances. I was there lying on my bunk, staring at the HVAC vents in the wall and fantasizing endlessly about unscrewing one and doing the Army crawl to freedom. Sharing that with the other women in my area caused an outburst of laughter.

It felt good to laugh.

It felt so good to be sober and FREE after seventeen years of being high.

From the depths of my brand-new, Christ-loving heart, I knew God had a plan for me. My circumstances couldn't have looked bleaker as I contemplated a seventeen-years-to-life sentence, but for the first time in my life, I was free on the *inside*, and I knew it!

And I was free all because of Jesus, who sacrificed His life for mine and forgave me, loved me, and rose from the dead for me when He left behind an empty tomb.

After Jesus' death, He rose again to life so I too could rise up out of death's grip and live. And on that January of 2001 I made up my mind to grab hold of the second chance at life that God had so graciously granted me and live it to the fullest.

I became a voracious reader of God's Word. I quickly filled the pages with highlighting, underlining, writing in the margins, and a big "WOW" next to every Scripture that jumped out and spoke to me about my life. The Holy Spirit was wooing me through the pages, the stories, the psalms, and the proverbs.

David made a statement in Psalm chapter eighteen that accurately describes my feelings about what Jesus did for me.

He reached down from heaven and rescued me;
he drew me out of deep waters. (Psalm 18:16)

Perhaps this powerful statement by David describes your journey too. Or maybe having God reach down from heaven and rescue you from drowning is something you've been *longing* for. And as you're reading this book, perhaps the Holy Spirit is tugging on your heart and saying, "I'm calling you *today* out of darkness, out of pain, out of misery, out of the life you're living, and out of sin and desperation into forgiveness, grace, mercy, joy, freedom, and a brand-new life."

No matter where you are in your journey—saved or unsaved—God can write a brand new chapter in your story. It's not too late for you!

ONE MIRACLE AFTER ANOTHER

Miraculously, I didn't go through any withdrawals in prison. God supernaturally sobered me up, and I never got the shakes or had even a moment of nausea. I had zero withdrawal symptoms! I did, however, still have a huge, gaping ulcer on the bottom of my only foot. It was still badly swollen and burning hot to the touch.

I put in an inmate request to see the prison doctor, and within a few days I was taken downstairs to medical. The moment the doctor laid eyes on my foot, he stated, "Your right leg is going to be amputated too. We just need to wait for gangrene to set in, which should be any time now. When that happens, we will send you out to the hospital for amputation."

The doctor didn't know that I had just given my life to Jesus and was reading the living, breathing, life-transforming, chain-breaking Word of God. I looked at the doctor square in the eyes and announced excitedly, "No! Jesus is going to heal me! I just gave my life to Him, and my Bible says that by His stripes I am healed."

The doctor laughed at me and sent me back up to the fifth floor with a prescription for antibiotics and a promise that as soon as gangrene set in I would be sent out to the hospital for the amputation of my right, and only remaining foot.

God has an uncanny, supernatural, amazing, sovereign way of putting the right people in your life for the right purpose at *just the right time.* A woman in the bunk directly across from me "just so happened" to be a professional physical therapist who had been trained in wound care. Like me, she too had just given her life to Jesus.

She asked to see my foot and immediately exclaimed, "I can help you! I took special medical training in wound debridement."

Immediately, she began to search in her locker and pulled out a razor. She broke it open and pulled out the blade and said, "This will work perfectly!"

I jumped on my bunk, took off my sock, and waited with pure trust and excitement. The six other women in our pod gathered around, all excited for me and for what God was about to do through that lady to help heal my foot.

As soon as she got started, I could tell she knew what she was doing. She carefully cut away the dead, infected flesh that surrounded the deep, gaping hole in my foot. After approximately ten minutes, she looked up at me and smiled saying, "There! Now that wound will be able to close up."

Next, the six other women in my Bible study group joined us and laid their hands on my leg. They began to pray for me with great faith that God would heal the wound and close the hole. Then every day—multiple times a day—I proclaimed out loud, "By the power of Jesus, my foot is healed!" And based on God's promise of our healing in the book of Isaiah I also proclaimed out loud, "By Jesus' stripes I am healed!"

> *But He was wounded for our transgressions,*
> *He was bruised for our iniquities;*
> *The chastisement for our peace was upon Him,*
> *And by His stripes we are healed.* (Isaiah 53:5 NKJV)

I read a book on healing that explained how this passage of Scripture in Isaiah reveals that my healing took place nearly two thousand years ago on the cross of Calvary—where Jesus died for our sins. That was when my healing was bought and paid for.

So every day I sat on my bunk, took off my sock, and turned my foot over. And holding it so I could see the bottom, I declared, "Lord, I know I still see a hole in my foot right now. But I also know your word says my foot has already been healed. And I know this hole in my foot just has to catch up to your promise in Isaiah. So I declare today that I trust you,

God. And I know and believe and declare that by Jesus' stripes my foot is healed!"

I made God a promise. I promised Him that as soon as the hole closed up in my foot and was completely healed, I would put in a request to go back to medical to show the doctor that Jesus healed me. And God came through in a miraculous way!

Every single day as I looked at the bottom of my foot, I could physically see the hole was filling in. Every day I could see fresh muscle and flesh growing back.

Adriana (that was her name) continued to remove the calloused and dead flesh around the edge of the hole. The callous seemed to grow back rapidly, almost overnight. She faithfully continued to debride the new callous, and the group of Christian inmates faithfully continued to pray for me.

Two months—sixty days—later, the hole had completely filled in with brand-new flesh. There was brand-new skin where the hole had been.

I filled out a request to go to Medical with great excitement. I couldn't wait to tell the doctor what Jesus had done. I was escorted down to Medical within a couple of days. On the request I filled out, I just wrote that I needed to be rechecked; I didn't state that my foot had been healed.

When Dr. Benjamin walked into the medical exam room, I smiled at him, took off my sock, and held my foot out so he could see the bottom and shouted, "LOOK AT THIS! Jesus healed my foot!"

He walked up close to me, eyes widening, looked at my foot, and promptly turned around and walked back out, shutting the door behind him.

Moments later, he came back in with a team of six other medical professionals. They all gathered around my foot as though it were the eighth wonder of the world. I could see the amazement in their eyes as they looked at my foot and then at one another. Finally, Dr. Benjamin came close to me and looked me right in the face and stated, "I know Jesus healed you, because THAT is a miracle!"

A NEW PERSON

Paul told the Corinthians that anyone who is in Christ is a new person.

> *So we have stopped evaluating others from a human point of view. At one time we thought of Christ merely from a human point of view. How differently we know him now! This means that anyone who belongs to Christ has become a new person. The old life is gone; a new life has begun!*
>
> (2 Corinthians 5:16-17)

From the moment I gave my life to Jesus, He began to change everything about me. He was transforming me from the inside out into the person I longed to be for so many years. The first thing Jesus took away was my potty mouth.

I used to cuss like a sailor—or a truck driver. I even made up new words. But the moment I surrendered my heart to Jesus, He gave me a new mouth. It was as though a sense of holy reverence, awe, and love flooded my heart and flushed out corruption.

The next thing Jesus did was take away my desire to look at anything inappropriate. The Holy Spirit helped me realize that I needed to—as Proverbs says—*"Keep* [my] *heart with all diligence, for out of it spring the issues of life*" (Proverbs 4:23 NKJV).

I realized that my eyes and my ears were the gateways to my heart, and I wanted to protect my heart with every ounce of strength and faith I had within me. Jesus died to give me a second chance and make me new, and I was determined that I was not going to put anything inside my heart that would bring poison to my soul that had been set free.

Whenever a TV program was on containing inappropriate material, like sexually suggestive scenes or foul language, and other inmates were watching it, it was as though the Holy Spirit was pulling me up out of the chair and pushing me right out of the room.

Other inmates began to notice that the one-legged lady who passionately loved Jesus was working hard to keep her heart pure. Those inmates came to me and started asking me about this Jesus whom I loved so much. They were noticing that I was a new person, and even in federal prison facing a life sentence, I had crazy, ridiculous joy.

I smiled constantly; I laughed often. The joy on the inside of me was so infectious that everyone around me wanted some of it. Even the correctional officers started asking me about my experience with Jesus. And a few of the guards who were Christians looked me right in the eye and said, "I can tell you've had a real experience with Jesus, because that joy on your face is unmistakable and real."

I felt as though I had grown angel's wings and could fly around the prison, so great was my joy! I was still facing seventeen years to life, but the joy, the love, the forgiveness, and the mercy of Jesus Christ had set me free, and no prison sentence could diminish my faith.

The Holy Spirit began to work with me to make me do the right thing even when no one was looking. He was not only my Comforter, He was my Teacher. When I walked by a piece of trash that someone had thrown on the ground, the Holy Spirit spoke to my heart instantly, "Julie, pick that up."

At first, aghast, I looked up and said, "Lord! That's not my trash; I didn't do that."

The Holy Spirit replied, "I'm not asking you if you did it. I'm telling you to go back and pick it up. I'm telling you to do the right thing when no one else is looking but me."

Instantly, tears filled my eyes as the conviction of the Holy Spirit pierced my heart. I turned around and picked up the piece of trash and headed straight for a trash can. The moment I obeyed the voice of the Holy Spirit, a deep sense of joy and purity flooded my entire being. I knew God was pleased with me, because I was listening to His voice and obeying Him.

Nothing was better than that! I discovered nothing feels better than obeying the voice of the Lord moment by moment throughout the day. I placed Him on the throne at the center of my life—that center around which everything revolved.

I read my Bible with unveiled eyes and heart, and I soaked up everything around me that had anything to do with Jesus. I was like a sponge as I dug into the Word and every Bible study I could find on the bookshelves of the prison library. One day I came across a poem that was written by Myra Brook Welch in 1921. The poem is called *The Touch of the Master's Hand* (it has also been called *The Old Violin*).

This poem resonated deep within my spirit, and by the time I read the last line, I was weeping uncontrollably, overcome by the goodness, love, and mercy of God toward me.

THE TOUCH OF THE MASTER'S HAND

'Twas battered and scarred, and the auctioneer
Thought it scarcely worth his while
To waste much time on the old violin,
But held it up with a smile.
"What am I bidden, good folks," he cried,
"Who'll start the bidding for me?"
"A dollar, a dollar. Then two! Only two?
Two dollars, and who'll make it three?"

"Three dollars, once; three dollars, twice;
Going for three . . . " But no,
From the room, far back, a grey-haired man
Came forward and picked up the bow;
Then wiping the dust from the old violin,
And tightening the loosened strings,
He played a melody pure and sweet,
As a caroling angel sings.

The music ceased, and the auctioneer,
With a voice that was quiet and low,
Said: "What am I bid for the old violin?"
And he held it up with the bow.
"A thousand dollars, and who'll make it two?
Two thousand! And who'll make it three?
Three thousand, once; three thousand, twice,
And going and gone," said he.

The people cheered, but some of them cried,
"We do not quite understand.
What changed its worth?" Swift came the reply:

"The touch of the Master's hand."
And many a man with life out of tune,
All battered and scarred with sin,
Is auctioned cheap to the thoughtless crowd
Much like the old violin.

A "mess of pottage," a glass of wine,
A game—and he travels on.
He is "going" once, and "going" twice,
He's "going" and almost "gone."
But the Master comes, and the foolish crowd
Never can quite understand
The worth of a soul and the change that is wrought
By the touch of the Master's hand.

I held the book containing Myra's poem close to my chest as I walked over to an old-fashioned typewriter that sat on a table in the prison library. One of the inmates gave me a plain white piece of paper. I sat down and carefully typed each word with tears streaming down my face the entire time.

Next, I borrowed a set of colored pencils, and I carefully drew a violin on the paper. Women in prison spend a lot of time coloring and creating pieces of handcrafted art to send home to their families. I wanted to send that poem and the picture I made to my mom to share with her that the Master had come, and the touch of His hand had wrought great change in my heart and life.

I knew it was probably too soon for my dear mother to readily believe I was a new creation, but I was so eager to let her know that her daughter was changing for the good, and that it was all because of Jesus Christ!

PASSING THE TEST

One day, volunteers came into the prison to provide the opportunity for inmates to take the GED test. Although I had graduated from high school and had my diploma, I decided to take the test, because after seventeen years of snorting methamphetamine up my nose and into my brain—and after drinking enough alcohol to preserve all the peaches in Georgia—I wanted to see if my brain could still function well enough to go to school.

I promised my mom I was going to go to correspondence school and get my bachelor's degree in prison. So I signed up to take the GED test, and I prayed with all my heart before I took it.

I placed my hands on the test paper and pleaded, "God, help me! I want to go to college. I want to make the most of the second chance at life you've given me. Please help me, Lord! Help me pass this GED test with flying colors. Show me, Father, if it's your will for me to go to college and get my degree. Help me, Lord, and give me favor with this test. I ask this in Jesus' mighty name. Amen."

Two weeks later, the volunteers came back to the prison with our test scores. Not only did I pass my GED test, I also passed it with the highest score! I literally jumped up and down with excitement. That was my sign from God. Not only had God restored my brain cells, He was giving me an opportunity to create a brand-new future that would include a bachelor's degree.

Oh, the precious blood of Jesus that washes away our sins and makes us new. Oh, the precious stripes of Jesus by which we are healed, redeemed, restored, renewed, and set free to live for him!

As you continue to read my story, I want you to know that *nothing* you face is impossible with God—NOTHING! The blood of Jesus has never lost its power. Jesus is the same yesterday, today, and forever (Hebrews 13:8). He loves you with an unfailing love. His mercies never fail. They are new every morning.

GREAT is His faithfulness! All it takes is a made-up mind that you are never going back to that old person again—back to those old destructive mindsets, back to that old life, or back to those old ways.

Once you get to the place where you are truly grieved in your heart over the person you have become, the life you are living, and the pit you are in, nothing can stop you from pursuing Jesus and overcoming every obstacle you face.

Nothing can stop you from choosing Jesus. And once you choose Jesus and give yourself over to His rule, *nothing* can stop Him from pouring into you an abundance of hope for your future in His service.

Chapter 7

THE BATTLE BELONGS TO THE LORD

EVEN THOUGH I was in federal prison, and even though an attorney had told me I made a fatal error when I kidnapped my son, I began to really believe that someday I would see Tyler again. The Lord had performed multiple miracles for me, the greatest of which was changing me into a new person, and I knew He could do anything.

CHOOSING TO BE COURAGEOUS

I had read in Psalm thirty-seven, "*Delight yourself also in the Lord, and He shall give you the desires of your heart. Commit your way to the Lord; trust also in Him, and He shall bring it to pass*" (Psalm 37:4-5 NKJV). And of course it was my desire to be free from incarceration. But most of all, I desired more than anything to see and hold my Tyler.

I realized if it was in God's plan to grant me the most significant desire of my heart, and if that day came when I was freed, I would have to face Tyler's dad in a courtroom again. I believed in order to see my boy, I would have to face a judge.

I also believed if that day ever came, I would have to come face to face—again—with my crimes, my addictions, my sinful life, my mistakes, and the fact that in the eyes of society I was considered nothing but hopeless, worthless, purposeless, useless trash!

What in the world was I to do? I had been put to shame during the custody battle in that small-town courtroom in Tennessee just before I took Tyler and fled to Mexico. My reprehensible, sinful life had been exposed before the courtroom audience, and I was gripped with fear over the thought of being publicly shamed again. Even though I knew I was a new person in Jesus Christ, I also knew that many who knew me "before Jesus" would not care a whit whether or not I had changed.

They would only want to see me humiliated and disgraced—again.

Despite my fear, I decided I would prepare myself for that day. I made up my mind to face whatever humiliation I had to face in order to get in front of a judge and ask permission to see my precious little boy again.

I made up my mind to be courageous.

It was right there in that federal prison where I developed the courageous faith to believe that God had plans for my life—for good and not evil—to give me hope and a future (Jeremiah 29:11). It was there in that federal prison where God sent that woman, a volunteer prison minister, to come to the fifth floor, sit on my bunk, and insist over and over to me that Jesus loved me, that He had been nailed to a cross and died for me, and that He would forgive me if I would repent of my sins and surrender my life to Him.

It was there in that federal prison where I read the words of Joshua 1:9 for the very first time: *"This is my command—be strong and courageous! Do not be afraid or discouraged. For the* Lord *your God is with you wherever you go."*

The tall, concrete block building in the center of downtown San Diego where I was imprisoned was supposed to be a place of confinement and punishment. But for me it became a place of freedom, sobriety, and a second chance at life. How ironic that man had built that building as a place to *protect* society from criminals—from me—but God had set me in that building to prepare me to be a *blessing* to society—a light in a dark world.

God used my incarceration to prepare me to be His light and share His truth in a world full of confusion and lies. I was set free from sin and darkness in that place of confinement. And in that place of confinement, chains and strongholds were forever removed from my life.

It takes courage to live beyond regrets, but the good news is that God wanted to take my mess and turn it into a miracle. The verses of Proverbs 3:5-6 became my way of life. They say, *"Trust in the* Lord *with all your heart; do not depend on your own understanding. Seek his will in all you do, and he will show you which path to take."*

In my private time of prayer and devotion there in prison, the Lord spoke to my heart, and many times I wrote down in my prayer journals what He said. Here's something He said to me and placed in my heart:

> Julie, you are going to need to be courageous. You will have to face your past, including people who wanted to destroy you. Yes, I've redeemed you and made you a new

creation, but you will need the courage to face people who don't believe in you, hold resentment against you, and will still try to tear you down based on who you used to be.

You will also need to be courageous, because life on earth is hard. You will experience loneliness, loss, temptation, rejection, and attacks. But do not fear, for I will be with you! My rod and staff will comfort you [Psalm 23:4].

You will live to see my goodness in your life right here in the land of the living [Psalm 27:13]. I will never leave you nor forsake you [Deuteronomy 31:6; Hebrews 13:5]. Though at times it will feel as though you are walking through the valley of the shadow of death, you need not fear [Psalm 23:4], for if you remain committed to me, I will comfort you, protect you, bless you, and keep you safe under the shelter of my wing [Psalm 91:1-4].

JESUS IN THE PRISON CELL

It was time for me to face my final sentencing, and I spent time discussing my future with my federal defender who represented me. She was an incredibly kind woman. She met with me several times and wanted to fight for me. She was even willing to go to trial to fight to get me off the charges. When she came to ask if I was absolutely *sure* of what I had been carrying, wrapped around my waist underneath layers of duct tape, the new *honest* Julie had to tell her the truth.

"Yes, I knew exactly what I was smuggling, and no, I do not want to go to trial."

I looked into her intelligent, caring eyes and not only told her that I knew what I was doing but also told her it was a reprehensible crime, and I wanted to stand before the judge and receive whatever sentence he gave me. I didn't want to lie to her or to the judge. I had put my faith and my life in the hands of God, and I fully trusted Him with the outcome.

In June of 2001, the day came for me to go to court for my sentencing. I had taken many trips, handcuffed, through the underground tunnel that goes from the Metropolitan Correctional Center in downtown San Diego to the courthouse across the street. And I was thankful that the United States Marshals never shackled me on any of those trips.

All of the other inmates were shackled, but the marshals didn't want to shackle me with my prosthetic leg, because I was already struggling to walk on it. The titanium screws holding the socket to the pylon, and the pylon to the foot, had recently started coming loose, and it shifted dangerously every time I stepped on it. I knew it was the grace of God holding my prosthesis together until I could get a new leg made.

My federal defender asked the judge if after sentencing I could serve my time at Federal Medical Center Carswell in Dallas, Texas. That was the prison where they sent inmates who had either mental health or medical issues. It was also the prison that had the five hundred-hour Residential Drug and Alcohol Program, and I was requesting the judge to issue a court order for me to participate in that program.

Since I had given my life to Jesus, I wanted to do everything possible to equip myself to live a life of victory, even from inside prison. My federal defender had already gotten my sentence down from seventeen-to-life to ten years. And she told me she was going to ask the judge for six and a half years on my sentencing day. But she also told me not to expect that to happen, because she wasn't sure the judge would approve it.

I was escorted to a cell located behind the courtroom. As they were locking the door behind me, the U. S. Marshals warned me, "You have the toughest judge in San Diego. You're in trouble. He is going to lock you up and throw away the key. Don't expect anything good to happen today."

The metal door locked with finality, and they walked away, leaving me alone in the cell.

Or so they thought.

I was nervous. My moment of reckoning had come. It was the moment I would stand before the judge in the federal court room and receive my sentence. I had already written the judge a letter that was presented to him by my federal defender. It was a letter apologizing for the repugnant crime I had committed. I told the judge that I had given my heart and life to Jesus and wanted to go to college, get my degree, and become a positive, productive person.

I told the judge I was looking forward to taking college correspondence courses from prison. And I let him know I was determined to get my bachelor's degree and make good use of my time of incarceration.

As I sat on the hard, cold metal bench, I leaned forward and began to pray. Tears filled my eyes as I told Jesus how much I loved Him and how grateful I was that He had rescued me from a life of certain death in Mexico. I told Jesus that no matter what, I would live for Him, that my life belonged to Him, and that He could do whatever He wanted to do with it.

As I prayed, the light in the cell increased. I looked at the empty metal bench across from me, and I saw a circle of light. And inside the light was a silhouette that looked like Jesus, or an angel!

Even as I am writing this book—almost twenty years later—the hairs on my arms are standing straight up. The Holy Spirit is bearing witness to me, even now, after all this time, that it was HIM in that cell with me that morning.

I knew God was right there with me in that prison cell. And I knew that whatever the outcome, it would only happen with God's stamp of approval. No sentence would be given to me except that which my precious Lord would allow, and He was going to remain right by my side every second.

As I prayed, I asked my heavenly Father for a second chance at life. I told Him that while I was planning to go to college in prison, I would really love the chance to get out in six and a half years and be able to enjoy life outside the razor-wire fence.

SENTENCING TIME

The marshals came to get me. They escorted me into the courtroom, and it was my turn to stand in front of the judge. I stood before that honorable judge six months earlier at my arraignment when he slammed the gavel down and pronounced my sentence of seventeen years to life with my mom sitting in the courtroom. On that day back then, I had on a very wrinkled, khaki prison jumpsuit. My hair was uncombed, and my face was blotchy from crying. I was a mess from head to toe.

I was a different woman standing before him the day of my sentencing. My hair was brushed and shiny because I had been able to purchase shampoo, conditioner, and a brush from the commissary. My khaki prison uniform was neat and crisply pressed with an iron. My eyebrows had been artfully shaped and threaded by one of the inmates who used the thread from the hem of a pair of prison pants.

I was clean and presentable, humble, and ready to receive my sentence with a spirit of thankfulness. I was ready to transfer to a real prison and start my college correspondence classes. I heard there was good food, recreational facilities, and great chapel services in the federal prisons.

I was ready to go and do my time!

The judge looked down at me from his majestic mahogany desk and told me he had reviewed my case and read my letter. He asked if I had anything to say to the court.

My knees were trembling as I stood before him and began to speak.

"Your Honor, I just want to say how truly sorry I am for the repugnant crime that I committed. I gave my life to Jesus here in prison, and I want to go to college and get my bachelor's degree. I recently took my GED test and passed with a very high score. I want to do everything I can to become a positive, productive member of society."

The judge listened, thoughtfully, watching my face as I spoke. I was honest and eager to share the *good* that was inside my *new* heart.

"I am going to give you a chance here," the judge announced. "I am going to give you the chance you are hoping for. I am sentencing you to thirty months in federal prison. You will only have to serve twenty-two of those months. And I want you to keep in touch with me! I want to hear how you're doing."

I couldn't believe my ears!

"Thank you! Thank you so much, your honor! Yes, I will keep in touch with you, I promise!"

The U.S. Marshals came to escort me out of the courtroom. My federal defender said the judge really took a chance on me, and she encouraged me to keep my promise and be sure to write to him to update him on my life.

I was going to serve only twenty-two months in federal prison! God kept His word to me! I recalled the moment I stood at the border six months earlier with methamphetamine duct taped around my waist, when the Lord spoke clearly to me.

"*Two years*," He said.

At one time, I thought God didn't know what the federal sentencing guidelines were for four pounds of meth. But I learned that day in the federal courtroom that God's plan simply trumps man's sentence. God's purposes trump man's predictions.

I learned that God makes a way where there seems to be no way (Isaiah 43:19). I learned that God really does want to take people's circumstances—and even their biggest mistakes—and use them for His glory by making a new creation, by giving them a second chance at life, and by demonstrating His grace, mercy, love, and power through them as they walk daily with Him hand in hand!

That day in the courtroom, God made His Word in Psalm chapter forty come to pass in my life.

I waited patiently for the LORD to help me,
and he turned to me and heard my cry.
He lifted me out of the pit of despair,
out of the mud and the mire.
He set my feet on solid ground
and steadied me as I walked along.
He has given me a new song to sing
a hymn of praise to our God.

Many will see what he has done and be amazed.
They will put their trust in the L*ORD*. (Psalm 40:1-3)

I was overcome with joy as I was escorted back to the Metropolitan Correctional Center through that underground tunnel. It was a surreal feeling to be a prisoner in handcuffs in the city I loved so much, so close to the ocean, and yet feel so much joy.

How truly grateful I had become for those handcuffs. I was grateful for my metal prison bunk and its thin mattress. I was thankful for my prison uniforms, white socks, and even federally issued underwear! I was grateful for every breath I took. I was thankful to be in a safe place that had given me food to eat and a place to sleep. And then, I became grateful beyond words for my second chance at life.

I, Julie Fitzpatrick, was going to get out of prison in less than two years and be FREE—free to live for Jesus, free to go to college on a real campus, and free to do all the good things with my life that I should have done years earlier.

By the grace of God, I was given a second chance to do all of them.

When it looks like we've lost all, a spirit of gratitude will propel us into God's blessings. I no longer woke up each morning thinking of dying or getting high. Yes, the pain of failing my beloved little boy was still excruciating, but the joy of my precious Lord was far greater. And that can only happen by God's supernatural power!

You see, when I gave my heart and life to Jesus and truly repented of my sins, God put His Spirit inside me. The Holy Spirit became my Comforter, my strength, and my guide. And the Spirit of God within me became greater to me than my failures, my prison sentence, and even the pain of separation from my only child. The feeling of experiencing God's love and mercy that I had then—and still have today—also surpassed the pain of the death of my dear dad.

Yes, all those things still hurt; I was not immune to pain. But I was walking courageously through painful situations, and I was discovering that God meant what He said as recorded in Deuteronomy 31:6 and quoted in Hebrews 13:5 when He declared, *"I will never fail you. I will never abandon you."*

As soon as I got back to my prison dorm, I went straight to the inmate telephones hanging on the wall, and I called my mom to tell her the good news and let her know it would not be long before I was transferred to Federal Medical Center Carswell, in Dallas, Texas.

Mom was ecstatic! She could tell something inside of me had really changed, and she said that once I was released, I could move back home and go to college. It then made more sense to me to attend college after I was released as opposed to enrolling in correspondence classes from inside a federal prison.

I told my mother about a wonderful rehabilitation program in prison called RDAP (Residential Drug and Alcohol Program), in which I could acquire the skills and learn the practical steps I would need to take in order to remain clean and sober for the rest of my life. I no longer wanted to go back to old habits or old friendships. I knew I needed to do everything differently and redo every aspect of my life.

Yes, I emphasized that the Holy Spirit was living inside of me, and spiritually speaking I was a brand-new person. But my flesh-and-blood body had used and abused substances for seventeen years, and I was determined to equip and empower myself with the necessary tools to walk in victory with my Jesus.

I had prayed diligently about being granted permission to enroll in the RDAP program. And miraculously, the judge recommended that I be allowed to complete the program during the remainder of my incarceration. I had just the right amount of time left. It became abundantly clear that the Lord was moving on the hearts of people in authority to ensure that I would have what I needed to live a successful, Spirit-filled life.

HEADING TO TEXAS

About one week after my sentencing day, my name was called by the federal marshals at 2:00 am when they came to pick up women for transport. Inmates are not given any warning or advance notice of their transportation date. That's done intentionally to prevent those outside of prison from hijacking the federal transport van in an attempt to help an inmate escape.

I had to leave behind all of my commissary food, coffee, Bible, and hygiene items I had purchased during my six month stay at MCC San Diego. I quickly gave it all away to inmates who swooped in like vultures, and with one last glance over my shoulder, I held out both hands in front of me as the U.S. Marshals cuffed me, escorted me out into the dark night, and loaded me into the waiting transport van.

I had heard great things about federal prison. MCC San Diego was only a holding facility, and once inmates received their final sentence from the judge, they're transported to a federal prison to do their time. The inmates I had met over the previous six months told me the food was excellent in federal prison. I had also heard tales of softball games, snow cone machines, and filet mignon on special holidays. I was dying to find out if it was all true.

The ride from San Diego to our first stop in Arizona took about five hours. I shifted continuously, trying unsuccessfully to find a comfortable position on the cold metal bench. My prosthetic leg had a broken release button and was in desperate need of replacement. And all of the wiggling around finally resulted in my prosthesis falling off. It made a loud clunking noise as it hit the floor of the van.

I leaned over and tried to grab it, but my handcuffs made it impossible. I slipped off the bench and ended up on the floor, wedged between the metal wall of the van and the seat. I was being transported with two other women, and we were squealing with laughter as they tried without success to pull me up off the floor.

Due to regulations, the federal marshals driving the van would not pull over even though they heard the raucous noise. As uncomfortable as the next hour was having to ride on the floor in that position, I just couldn't stop smiling. The Lord knew we needed laughter in that moment, and what might have been a somber event turned into a time of lighthearted camaraderie between us three inmates in the front row.

After five hours, we stopped at a little county jail in a small rural town somewhere in Arizona. It was a holding place of sorts while we were on the road to the federal prison in Texas. I sat in that little jail for what seemed like the longest four weeks of my life. I had no money and was not able to make any phone calls to let my mom know where I was.

I was given a thin bar of soap that smelled like old socks to use during my four week stay. Desperate to wash my hair, I gave in and used the soap since it was all I had. Afterward, my hair felt like old, fragile straw and hung limply in matted strands around my face. After a few days, I was given a cheap toothbrush—but no toothpaste. Toothpaste was considered a luxury. And since my prosthesis was in need of repair, I was forced to "walk" in a bent-over position until they provided me with crutches.

The days and nights went by slowly. Waiting for the next federal transport van was like watching a pot of water on a medium burner and waiting for it to boil. One night after dinner, three other inmates and I were notified that we would be transported by the feds sometime during the night. As I waited, a deep sadness came over me, and I was bombarded with "what if" thoughts.

"What if God really *doesn't* forgive me?"

"What if God is mad at me, and I only *think* I'm forgiven?"

"What if there really *isn't* a hope and a second chance for my life?"

"What if God doesn't *really* love me?"

"What if I really *did* mess up my life beyond repair?

I asked God (silently, in my head) if He really forgave me. I was scared—no, I was terrified at the thought that the magnificent, loving, benevolent, gracious God with whom I had fallen so deeply in love might actually be angry with me and refuse to forgive me.

"God, have you really forgiven me? Do you really love me? How can I know that you really have forgiven me? Lord! I need to know. Please speak to me. I need you, God!"

A tear slid down my face, and I lowered my head to the metal table, resting it on a Bible that I had rescued and adopted from an old dusty bookshelf in the open two-story jail pod.

Suddenly, the Lord said, "Julie! Don't put your head on it, open it up and read it!"

"What? Am I imagining this?" I wondered.

I raised my head and pushed the Bible open with my right hand, allowing it to fall open to the first place it seemed to want to go. My eyes fell immediately on a Scripture in Second Chronicles, and as I read that Scripture, my heart jumped for joy!

> *Then if my people who are called by my name will humble themselves and pray and seek my face and turn from their wicked ways, I will hear from heaven and will forgive their sins and restore their land.* (2 Chronicles 7:14)

"That's ME, God! Oh, my Father!" I shouted in my own mind. "This is talking about ME! Julie! I humbled myself and sought your face. I turned from my wicked ways and surrendered my life to you. And you heard the cry of my heart just now. You knew I needed this exact verse at this very moment to reassure me that you *have* forgiven me of my sins!"

We were taken from the jail to the airport and put on a plane for our transport to Texas. The early morning flight from Arizona to Texas took less than three hours. During the flight I was struck by the personal significance of the bright orange sunrise streaming through the airplane window and splashing across my face.

A new day, a new season was beginning for me.

I was about to serve the remaining sixteen months of my time at the federal medical center. I was in dire need of a new prosthetic leg, so the judge had approved my request to be sent to that facility. I was thrilled about that, and I was also excited about the prospect of entering the nine-month Residential Drug Abuse Program. I was about to get a new leg *and* free drug abuse rehab!

Upon arrival, I couldn't help but look around in awe as I was escorted, still in handcuffs, through the chain-link fence onto the prison compound in Fort Worth, Texas. It was huge! It covered one hundred and three acres to be exact, and it was enclosed by a twelve foot security fence with multiple coils of thick, gleaming razor wire to prevent escape attempts.

After a full strip search performed by female officers at the inmate intake area, my cuffs were removed, and I was taken to my new home.

The imposing two-story, barrack-style building was big enough to land a plane in. It was open in the center and lined with rooms around the perimeter of both floors. The individual rooms held two metal bunk beds with four-inch mattresses instead of the thin two-inch mats in Arizona and San Diego.

Each inmate got her very own large, military-style locker. There was an enormous, clean bathroom on the first floor with multiple shower stalls and hot running water—a luxury I had sorely missed. And the food . . .! The inmates were served real food like pasta, salad, steak, chicken, and Mexican food as compared to the smashed sandwiches and quarter-sized flavorless cookies served in the holding prisons.

I was very poor in the San Diego facility since my disability checks had been stopped when I was arrested. But in Texas I was given the opportunity to get a job on the prison grounds and earn my own money to buy real shampoo along with other much needed and coveted hygiene items.

I was able to buy coffee, soup, and snacks. And I put money on my inmate phone account to call my mom. Later, I had the ability to purchase a thick, plush, white terry bathrobe, a soft pair of grey sweatpants with a matching sweatshirt, and new white Nike tennis shoes—ALL paid for by real money that I earned by working!

GETTING A REAL JOB

It was one of my roommates who told me about a job working at UNICOR. UNICOR is a correctional program on the prison grounds where inmates make products or provide services while being equipped with job skills that could be put to use after their release from prison. And the job my roommate told me about was not just any job. It was the most coveted job in the entire prison, with a starting pay rate of $1.37 an hour!

"Lord! That's exactly what I need, Lord!" I started praying as soon as I was told about the job.

"I haven't asked anyone to send me any money for hygiene items, stamps, coffee, or phone calls since I've been in prison. I've been trusting in you to provide for my every need, and I'm now asking you, Father, to bestow favor on me and roll out a red carpet for this UNICOR job!"

The next day, while walking around the prison grounds during free time I turned my head and saw the UNICOR building right in front of me. I stopped and stared at the sign and the tinted-glass entrance doors. Putting one foot—or maybe I should say, one leg—slowly in front of the other, I started to walk nervously toward the entrance.

I had no idea if I could qualify for the job that consisted of processing government patents on a computer. I'd heard there was a minimum typing speed required of thirty-five words per minute, and I couldn't type—at all. But I put my faith and trust in a Savior who told His disciples, *"Humanly speaking, it is im-*

possible. But with God everything is possible" (Matthew 19:26). In my mind, "everything" had to mean . . . "Every Thing!" And in this case it had to mean my ability to type thirty-five words per minute.

I opened the door and stepped inside while trying to hide the fact I was nervous.

"Hi, I'm here to take the typing test and apply for a job at UNICOR," I said with as much confidence as I could muster.

Ten minutes later I was sitting at a computer with my heart racing and palms sweating as I typed as fast as my two index fingers could go. Sixty seconds flew by, and the kind officer who had ushered me in to take the test, returned to check on me.

Thirty-three words! I was two words short.

The officer must have seen the crushed look on my face, and she immediately said, "That's okay. Try it one more time."

I was getting a second chance!

I passed the test the second time by typing thirty-seven words per minute. God gave me favor, and the officer gave me a work approval form to take back to my unit showing that I was approved to begin working at UNICOR the following morning.

Praise the Lord! To my God be ALL the glory!

My typing gradually improved. My work contained few if any errors. I was taking pride in my work; and I felt the excitement of having a real job. One Friday my name was even announced as Employee of the Week—ME, Julie Fitzpatrick! As I stood to my feet and walked up to accept the certificate from the UNICOR officer, a brand-new, never-before-felt joy washed over me. In that moment, I realized the satisfaction that comes from doing *hard* things the *right* way.

•

As an addict, I stole money from my parents to buy drugs; and experiencing the new, powerful joy of earning my own money and buying things with it provided to me a wonderful boost of confidence. And it reassured me that the day would come after my release when I would truly be able to work and become a productive member of society

Another significant blessing I received while in the Texas prison was my new prosthetic leg that took the specialist only four weeks to fit and fabricate. I was delighted that it fit so perfectly, and I didn't even require the usual series of adjustments needed when an amputee gets a new leg. Mine fit perfectly the very first time I tried it on.

That was truly another miracle from God, and I made sure to thank everyone responsible—from the prosthetic specialist to the warden of the prison. I wanted everyone to know how grateful I was for my new leg. I had read in my Bible a story about how when Jesus healed ten lepers, only one of them returned to thank Him (Luke 17:11-19). The new Julie wanted to be like that one leper, thankful for every good thing that came my way.

Life was so good! I had a great job. I had a new leg. And I was clean, sober, and healthy for the first time in seventeen years. It mattered not to me that I was on the wrong side of the razor-wire fence. I was sober, happy, and—even in prison—free. I was learning what it meant to be productive, work for a paycheck, and provide for my needs. It felt good to recognize my progress and have accomplishments to be proud of.

I suddenly remembered the vision that came to me so long ago in my parents' house. In that vision I was in prison, but I was happy, healthy, whole, and—best of all—at peace.

I had seen the "Julie" I so longed to be, and finally I WAS that Julie!

Imprisoned behind razor-wired walls, just as God had revealed, I realized that I was finally—really—FREE! With each passing day I became more confident that I would actually be able to thrive upon my release from prison. I would keep that bachelor's-degree promise I made to my mother.

I called Mom weekly to share my progress and joyfully plan my release. She sent me Hallmark cards for my birthday, and inside them were pictures cut out from a catalogue of the actual clothes she had already purchased for me. Mom finally believed in the change that was happening in my life. She could hear my sincerity as I gushed about my relationship with Jesus, and she believed I was really changing.

Chapter 8

THE PROGRAM THAT CHANGED MY LIFE

AFTER A SEVEN-MONTH wait, the day arrived when my name came to the top of the waiting list for the drug program. I packed my things eagerly and moved to the second floor of a six-story building that had formerly been a military hospital. I was with a new group of twenty women entering the RDAP program.

The reward for successful completion of the program was the reduction of a prison sentence by up to a full year. I didn't have enough time remaining in my sentence to get a year off. But I had just enough time to complete the program.

Some of the women were confused and asked me why I would intentionally put myself through the program's intensive therapy, strict schedule, and stringent program rules when I could have just stayed in my previous housing dorm, worked at UNICOR, led a simpler life, and gotten out of prison on the same release day.

I explained to each one that although I had given my heart and life to Jesus Christ and was now a Christian, I still needed to learn on a practical level how to navigate life on a daily basis through trials, disappointments, and hardships.

I needed to learn through the program why I had gone so far astray for so many years and why I made poor choice after poor choice when I was an intelligent woman capable of so much more. I told them how much I was looking forward to discovering practical strategies that would help me stay clean and sober and prepare me to be the mother that my son, Tyler, deserved to find one day.

I had dreams about Tyler every night. I was searching for him and couldn't find him. Then, suddenly, I could see him in a pool with huge waves crashing over him. He was drowning, and in my dream I was helpless and couldn't reach him. I woke up from those dreams grief-stricken and tormented with shame and despair over my failure to provide Tyler with a stable, substance-free home and the love of a sober, engaged, and nurturing mother.

Yes, I had surrendered my heart and life to the Lord in prison. I was a brand-new person in Christ Jesus according to God's promise in 2 Corinthians 5:17. But being a Christ-follower didn't make me suddenly immune to the pain or the reality of my poor life choices that left my innocent little boy in the wake of my emotional and psychological destruction.

In the midst of that immense pain, I knew the only way out of it was to push *through* it—to keep moving forward and partner with God as He worked to change me into the mother He originally created me to be. So I chose to push through pain. I chose to walk with God and trust Him to heal me and restore my son in His perfect timing and plan. I knew the RDAP program along with my personal, daily relationship with Jesus held the keys to lifelong sobriety. I needed everything that program had to offer.

The program structure consisted of a half day of classes, a half day at my job with UNICOR, individual therapy, and group therapy. Right before classes began each morning there was a community meeting in which women in the program would "call out" any women who had not been complying with program rules or who had been behaving in a way that was considered to be disrespectful to others.

The "called out woman" had to leave her seat and sit in a chair at the front of the room while the inmates took turns standing up and telling her exactly what her wrongdoing and misbehavior was. The woman in the "hot seat" was not allowed to speak, react, or respond in any way to what the women were telling her; she had to listen respectfully and then go back to her seat and quietly process the information. While humiliating, that process taught us that we all are responsible to our community and to society.

We learned there were consequences for wrong behavior, and we had to answer to the entire community for not following the rules or for treating someone with malicious intent, disrespect, or a lack of kindness. The prize moments came on those mornings when a woman who had previously been placed in the chair raised her hand and asked to return to the chair with permission to speak.

On those occasions, a woman expressed her heartfelt apologies and acknowledged her wrongdoing. She thanked the group for calling her out and shared how by doing it they helped her to change. The community then responded favorably to that and warmly praised the woman for her progress. That taught us both the reward of owning our mistakes and the value of doing difficult things the right way.

The program curriculum included a set of workbooks with readings and assignments. In the pages of my workbooks I was introduced to *Cognitive Behavioral Therapy* for the first time in my life. I learned I had faulty core beliefs that in turn caused unhealthy, automatic thoughts and cognitive distortions. And that led to dysfunctional behavior.

In layman's terms, I learned that my own *stinkin' thinkin'* is what got me into trouble!

I dove into the hard work of changing my behavior by changing the way I think. Light bulbs started coming on in the cerebral cortex of my brain as I completed my worksheets and recognized the unhealthy thought patterns that had held me captive for so long. It was time to break free from them.

I believed negative things about myself for many years. I was worthless, stupid, disgusting, fat, and the list goes on. And as I moved painstakingly through my workbooks, I had to identify and write down the people and events that played a role in the formation of those faulty beliefs. Vivid memories of the long string of men who had abused me physically, mentally, and emotionally ran rampant through my mind as I tried desperately to corral them, put them in writing, and leave them there on the page.

It hurt to relive the abuse and the words that had been hurled into my heart and mind where they made their home for so many years. Drinking and drugs helped me numb the pain inflicted by those people and events. But I knew I was finally getting to the bottom of my faulty core beliefs, and it was becoming easy to see how those beliefs had affected my thought processes and behavior. And when I realized my core beliefs could be changed once they were identified, I felt something new bubble up from within me.

A new sense of joy and empowerment!

Many of my core-belief changes that I carefully wrote down in my RDAP workbooks were statements that had come straight out of the Bible. The Word of God is what I used to change my negative thought patterns into healthier, more positive ones. I began replacing thoughts such as, "I am worthless; I can't do anything right," with, "I was bought with a high price, the precious blood of Jesus. I have immense value, and I can do all things through Christ who gives me strength!"

Another negative thought I changed was, "I will never be successful in life. I am already thirty-seven years old. It's too late for me." I replaced that with what God says about me in Jeremiah 29:11. "God has good plans for me, for a hope and a future. Therefore, it is not too late for me to live a meaningful, successful life of great purpose!"

Since God's Word is true and powerful, I knew I was changing my thought patterns and core beliefs to line up with something that was true, sure, and trustworthy.

There were times when retraining my brain was hard work. As part of my "changing" process, I began spending time with the Lord early in the morning every day with the intention of building a new habit that would become a strong foundation to support my new life with Jesus.

I purchased an obnoxious bell-style alarm clock that was sure to wake me every morning. And as soon as it did, I quickly got up, made a hot, delicious cup of coffee, and sat quietly in the day room with my Bible, my journal, and my Jesus.

Those were precious times of connecting with God, pouring out my heart to Him, and listening for His voice as He spoke to my heart. I knew that was something I would need to do forever in order to cultivate a strong, ongoing relationship with Jesus.

Every time I called my mom, I was eager to share the new things I was learning. It took me a while to convince her that federal prison was truly one of the best things that had ever happened to me. At first, she couldn't see prison as being a good thing, but I kept reassuring her that, through it, God rescued me and saved my life.

Eventually she came into agreement with me as I spoke openly to her about my addiction for the first time after lying about and trying to hide it from her for years. God blessed me with the opportunity to tell her how truly sorry I was for the pain I had caused her.

To which she enthusiastically exclaimed, "Oh, Hon! Don't worry about that. You're doing GREAT now! By the way, did I tell you I just bought you a new outfit? It's hanging in your closet waiting for you!"

Our phone conversations were a highlight of my new life, and I couldn't wait to get out of prison, go to college, and live for Jesus—all while my mom would have a front row seat to watch the miraculous changes God was making in my life!

Chapter 9

FACING LIFE WITHOUT MOM

IT WAS MAY 22, 2002. I was working in the computer lab when I was called up to the desk of the corrections officer. She had just hung up the phone and stood still, staring directly into my eyes.

"The Chaplain wants to see you," she stated.

A hundred thoughts flew through my head at once.

"The Chaplain doesn't know me. This is a huge prison. There are thousands of women here," I thought as my mind raced. "Why would he call for me? Something has happened! Oh, dear God, help me!"

I felt my arms and hands begin to tingle. My peripheral vision grew black, and suddenly I could only see in front of me as though I were looking through a tunnel.

"Snap out of it," the officer demanded. "Everything is fine."

She then called up another inmate—my friend, Lorraine—and said, "I want you to go with Ms. DeVere-Fitzpatrick to the chaplain's office."[2]

---

2 Notice the hyphen between my middle name, *DeVere*, and my last name, *Fitzpatrick*. The Federal Bureau of Prisons made an error when putting my name in their records, and for the length of my imprisonment and dealings with them following my release, they insisted on using *DeVere* as part of my last name.

In the pit of my stomach, I knew something was very wrong. I took a deep breath and closed my eyes.

"It's okay, Julie. It's going to be okay," I reassured myself.

I smiled gratefully at Lorraine, and we walked together across the prison compound to the chaplain's office. I forced myself to think of the best possibilities.

"Perhaps my mom called the prison and just wants to talk to me about something important. Perhaps she just wants to discuss my future plans and how I'm going to live with her once I get out of prison in six months. Maybe she's worried because my letter didn't make it to her house."

We arrived at the chaplain's office and knocked on the door, and as we waited in the hallway we made awkward small talk about the weather. The weather in Texas was sunny and beautiful. My mom's birthday had just passed, and I wondered if she had received my birthday card. I thought perhaps that's why she was calling.

The chaplain's door opened, and an inmate walked out. The chaplain asked me my name, and when I told him, he told me to come in—alone. And after I entered the office he shut the door behind us.

I stood in front of him, holding my breath, almost willing him to give me good news. His office was very small, and it seemed to be closing in on me.

"Do you have a mother named Marge Fitzpatrick?" He asked.

"Yes," I answered, not even recognizing my own voice.

"Well—she just died in her sleep," he announced.

"Oh God! NO!" I screamed as I covered my face with my hands and crumpled to the floor. "This cannot be happening!" My worst nightmare had come true.

I felt him pat me on the shoulder as though he were petting a dog. "I know it hurts, doesn't it?" he said.

I could tell he must have done that many times, because his words sounded routine and hollow. He asked if I wanted to call my family, and I said, "Yes."

He dialed my sister's phone number while he explained that my brother-in-law had been the one who called the prison to give him the news.

There was no answer. He looked at me and said, "I'm sorry. You can come back to my office, and we will try to call again in a few days."

"A few days? A few days may as well be eternity!" I exclaimed to myself in my spirit. "What happened to my mom? Was there an accident? Was she sick and she didn't tell me when we talked on the phone? I just talked to her three days ago!

"Dear God, she was so excited when I told her I had given my life to Jesus and was going to go to college and get my bachelor's degree. LORD! I asked you to keep her alive so she could see the change in me once I was released from prison. I wanted her to see me live for you and go to college and do all the things I promised her I would do! Oh Lord, HELP me!"

When I opened the door to leave, Lorraine was gone.

I walked out of the building into the bright, warm sun and looked up at the brilliant blue sky. Sunlight reflected off the razor wire fence that enclosed the prison while tears of shock and grief rolled uncontrollably down my face.

"How could the sun be shining now? The sun should in no way be shining. My mom is dead. Now I really have nobody left in this world."

There was an outdoor recreational area on the prison grounds with a quarter mile outdoor running track next to a softball field, and the corrections staff allowed me to go walk around the track so I could process the news. Because of my security level, I would not be allowed to attend my mom's funeral, which was fine with me since I dreaded the idea of attending wearing my khaki prison uniform, handcuffs, and shackles in front of my sisters and our long-time family friends.

Scenes from my life played like a video in my head. All the happier memories of my childhood came flooding back as I walked numbly around the track. I saw myself in my little yellow Sunday school dress that my mom had sewn herself. My sister and I had matching dresses, and our dad took us to get ice cream after church. Oh, how much my little sister and I looked forward to our family *Thrifty* ice cream trips!

I remembered the time I was in fifth grade and my mom had to alter a pair of my pants for school. During class, I looked down in horror to discover that the seams of my pants were unraveling! My pants literally came apart at the seams, starting at my waistband and going all the way down the inside and outside of both legs.

I spent part of the morning frantically borrowing a few sweaters from my classmates. I tied them around my waist and both thighs so the world would not see my underwear. Finally, I went to the principal's office to ask if I could go home. I felt *so* embarrassed.

The principal called Mom, mumbled something to her, and hung up the phone. With a strange look on her face, she told me I was allowed to go ahead and walk home from school. We lived in a nice neighborhood by the school, so—with all the sweaters securely tied around me—I started off on the half-mile trek to my house. It was the longest half mile of my life!

With each step I took, the sweaters loosened. So I had to stop every few steps and tighten them. But I finally got home. When I got to our house, I walked up to the front door and rang the doorbell. Mom opened the door, looked me up and down, and burst into hysterical laughter. She laughed so hard that tears streamed down her face as she leaned against the doorway, holding her sides.

Eventually realizing the hilarity of the situation, I laughed too. That became a famous story shared at holiday meals with our aunts, uncles, and cousins. Everyone knew not to let our mom do their clothing alterations.

As childhood memories came to the surface of my mind, so did the guilt from my adult years. I knew it had to be especially heartbreaking for my mom to have watched me go through my years of addiction, lying, stealing, and immorality.

So much grief, discouragement, helplessness, sadness, and embarrassment had to have plagued her mind and emotions. And yet, when I was in prison—when I called and told mom all about how I gave my life to Jesus and my plans to go to college to become the successful woman she knew I could become—my mom chose to believe in me!

She chose to HOPE! After months of phone calls and conversations, she knew in her heart that her daughter had finally changed. The pain of losing her would have been unbearable for me if she had died not knowing how I had changed. I gave her hope, and God gave me time to make amends.

In the vision God gave me so long ago now, He revealed to me that neither of my parents would be alive to see the change in me with their own eyes, but He graciously allowed me to explain the change to my mother during my telephone calls from prison. That was one of His greatest gifts to me, and for it, I will be eternally grateful.

I was heartbroken, but in my grief I determined that I couldn't let her down, and I couldn't let God down either—not after He gave His Son and His life for me! Too much was at stake. It was time to start doing the right thing.

This is what happens when you go through tragedy WITH Jesus instead of without Him. He gives you the desire, the strength, the courage, and the power (His power) to walk through *the valley of the shadow of death* and come out on the other side shining like the Son!

When we're determined to not allow our faith and our dreams to be crushed by regret, grief, and sorrow, God will be able to use our grief and sorrow to make us strong and increase our faith in Him.

MY NEXT STEP

That evening after dinner I got down on my knees in front of my metal bunk. None of my roommates spoke to me; they didn't know what to say. I felt so alone. Yet somehow in the midst of that aloneness, I knew Jesus was close by. I felt His presence surround me as I began to talk to Him.

"Father, what am I going to do now?" I whispered—raw, desperate, and broken.

Immediately, and as clear as a bell, the Lord spoke to my heart. "It's time to depend only on me now, Julie!" He answered.

He was still with me! My beloved Jesus was right beside me!

That morning I had just read Joshua 1:9, where God says, *"This is my command—be strong and courageous! Do not be afraid or discouraged. For the Lord your God is with you wherever you go."*

Greatly encouraged, I climbed back onto my metal bunk, grabbed my Bible, and pulled it to my chest tightly. That was how I slept every night, huddled under my scratchy grey prison blanket with both arms wrapped around my chocolate-brown leather Bible. Many times I held it close to my pillow and went to sleep with my cheek resting against its tear-stained cover.

I met with my drug program counselor the next morning. "I'm worried about you," he said. "You're looking very raw."

My face was splotchy from the sudden burst of tears that came, unannounced, every hour. Even though I felt Jesus with me, grief still washed over me in regular waves.

"My mom! My dear mom, who has never seen me do anything but mess up my life, is now never going to see me live for Jesus," were the words that ran through my mind.

"I am leaving to go home for the weekend," my counselor told me. "Are you going to be okay? Are you having any thoughts of suicide?"

"I'll be okay," I said.

As he handed me a book on grieving and told me to read it, I felt as though he was handing me a knife and pushing it into my heart. The acceptance of the book was another fresh moment of realization that my beloved mother was really gone.

I didn't want to read it. But I went back to my room and opened the book as the tears began to flow yet again. I only got through five pages before I had to put it down, convinced that the pain of reading the book was greater than the grief itself.

Eventually, though, I reopened the grief recovery book given to me by my drug program counselor. In the first few pages, the author suggested something I will never forget as long as I live. I had to get an index card and write on it the following statement:

"I, Julie Fitzpatrick, have the courage to face life without my mom."

The author instructed the reader to tape the index card someplace where it could be seen every day. And those words were to be repeated out loud every time the reader saw it. That exercise struck a chord deep inside my heart. That's what I needed—the courage to face life and still go on living *without my mom.*

It would take courage to live beyond regrets. I had a mountain of devastating regrets, but I also had Jesus, through whom I had the ability to overcome every single one of them and walk in wholeness.

I immediately went on a scavenger hunt to secure an index card. In ten minutes I had a nice crisp, new, white index card in my hand. I sat down at the same table in the common area where I read my Bible each morning and slowly, with great care and purpose, wrote the words that would give me the strength to move forward in the face of deep loss.

"I, Julie Fitzpatrick, have the courage to face life without my mom."

I stared at the index card for a while in disbelief, but then I realized I *had* to believe it. I realized I had to reach deep inside and find the strength to *keep* the promise I made to my mother. Almost weekly during our phone calls, I promised her that as soon as I got out of prison I would go to college and get my bachelor's degree. A vision played across my mind of walking across a platform at a university graduation and accepting my diploma in honor of her.

That was it! I made up my mind at that very moment that I was really going to do it. I was going to keep my promise.

I, Julie Fitzpatrick, was going to get my bachelor's degree, and no devil in hell was going to stop me!

When lunch time came, I didn't go to the cafeteria and eat like I usually did. Instead, I went back to my room to pray. My other roommates were all off working in various parts of the prison, so I had the room to myself. I shut the door, and I began to pray out loud.

"God, I want to do something good with my life. God, I want to stay clean and sober. I'm scared, Lord! I don't want to go back to using drugs or drinking alcohol ever again, but God, I don't know how to live as a sober person, so I'm going to need you to help me from the moment I open my eyes in the morning to the moment I lay my head down at night.

"God, I want to get out of prison and go to college. So Lord, I'll need a place to live, clothes to wear, a car to drive, and money for college. And Lord! I want to get my degree in order to secure a good job, get my own place, and become a positive, productive member of society.

"And God! I want my son, Tyler, back in my life. God, if you can do all of these things, it will be a miracle bigger than the parting of the Red Sea!"

I then sat down cross-legged on my prison bunk. Looking up, I could see all around the inside perimeter of the bunk above me the Scriptures that I had taped there to memorize. They weren't just random Scriptures; they were the verses that God told me I should pray over and hang on to. He was going to make them come to pass in my life if I would just keep pressing forward with Him and never give up.

I was hiding His Word in my heart as I started at one corner of the bunk and read each Scripture out loud. I did that every single day during my lunch break, and as I did, I discovered that faith comes by *hearing* the Word of God (Romans 10:17). I *read* the Word every day, and I *spoke* the Word out loud every day over my life and circumstances. And as I did, my faith in God's Word became unshakeable.

Even though my circumstances were not changing instantly, I felt things shifting in the supernatural realm as I spoke God's Word out loud and claimed His promises. And I knew God was actively working behind the scenes on my behalf.

MOM'S LETTER

My eyes widened when I heard my name called during the evening mail distribution. Nobody ever wrote to me. Nobody, that is, except my mother. I felt my legs start to buckle as I walked up to the front of the line. With my hands trembling, I took the letter the guard handed me.

It was from her! It was a letter from my mom. She had to have written it and put it in the mail right before she died. It took extra time for inmates to get mail because it all had to be read first by the corrections staff prior to delivering it to us.

I slowly opened the letter with trembling hands. I was going to relish every word of it.

> Hi Hon—
>
> Got your letter today while I was just getting ready to write you one. Yours was very interesting and am so glad to hear you are pointing your life in such a positive direction. I have been thinking about what you said in your last two letters and our most recent phone calls. Given the attitude that you are expressing now—I think you could achieve and become anything you want. You are blessed with a wonderful intellect, and by simply

applying a practical and methodical approach to allow for your physical problems, I know you can succeed. Some people are late bloomers—but bloom they do! It's time to bloom Sweetheart!!!

As far as staying with me being a "cop-out" or "taking the easy way out"—I beg to differ. It would be quite symbiotic—I assure you. Definitely, a 2-way street. I expect to gain from it as well as you. I could enumerate all the ways—but I don't care to share my feelings with anyone else, and I know your mail is read. Mostly—it would be a joy to see you blossom into the beautiful intelligent woman dad and I always knew you were capable of becoming.

Much Love—

Mom

PS—Julie—these are all things I wanted to say to you privately and face to face. But I feel it's important for you to hear them now and throw them into the mix when you are making your decisions.

With great care, I folded the letter, slipped it back into its envelope, and placed it in my Bible. I had a plan for that letter.

GOD'S MIRACULOUS MESSAGE

The grief continued to come in waves. The federal corrections officer in charge of my unit on the fourth floor said I didn't have to go to work, but I wanted to go because I didn't want to be alone to think. I needed the distraction.

As I walked to the table to pick up a patent for processing on the computer, the officer in charge looked up at me and said, "You don't look well. Do you want to go back to your room?"

"No," I replied with tears in my eyes. Always those tears—it seemed I was crying constantly every day.

She stared at me again, and reaching down to the bottom of the stack, she pulled out a very thin folder. That manila folder was only one-quarter-inch thick at the most, and it contained only twenty-two pages to be exact. That was not only surprising to me, but it was also extremely unusual, because the government patents I had previously worked on were always huge—in folders two to three inches thick, containing a perfectly type-written patent/invention.

In my work, as I pulled up each patent on the computer, a scanned copy of the patent came up on the computer screen, and I went through the patent, page by page, and carefully edited what was on the computer screen so it matched the paper copy in the folder.

The paper copy had been carefully typed by the inventor and had no errors. Normally, the electronic version had *many* errors, at least fifteen per page. The errors were either typos or random apostrophes, dashes, or commas in places they were not supposed to be. My job was to make all the necessary corrections. The corrected patent was then sent to the government to become an official patent for whatever the invention or product was.

I had never seen a folder as thin as the one I held in my hand. I opened the manila folder and set the paper patent on a stand so I could look at it while I was typing. Then I turned on my computer.

As the scanned version of the patent came up on my computer screen, I placed my hands on the keyboard, ready to start correcting. I felt like I was about to have a breakdown. Grief had a hold on me like a vice grip, and I was trembling as

I felt the tears flowing once again. I was an emotional wreck. I missed my mom desperately, and I was cut off from all family. Her death was surreal yet excruciatingly *real* at the same time.

Suddenly my eyes grew wide, and the tears came to a stop. My computer screen was full of Scriptures from the Bible!

"This isn't a patent!" I thought as my mind raced. "It can't be. It's the Word of God!"

On my monitor were Scriptures from the Psalms about how God comforts us in times of sorrow and heals our broken hearts. What I read on the screen was almost like a Bible study about God's love for me and His promises to comfort and carry me through every sorrow I would ever face in life.

I jumped up from my chair and called out to the other inmates around me.

"Come here. Look! God is talking to me on my computer!"

In that moment, every bit of sorrow melted away, and I was suddenly smiling, even laughing, with a mixture of wonder and disbelief.

"Can this really be happening? Am I actually seeing this? God! Oh Father! it's YOU. I know it! You are HERE. You see me!"

Seven inmates surrounded my computer. They confirmed what I was seeing. They saw it too, and we all were in awe. How could something like that happen? It had to be God doing it. And it was a miracle.

Mary, one of the inmates who held me accountable in my walk with Jesus, said excitedly, "Julie! Don't correct the mistakes. Leave a lot of mistakes so that you can get it back tomorrow and read it again!"

That was how the patent process worked. If we didn't correct all the mistakes, we would get the patent back the next day so we could finish correcting it.

"What a great idea!" I agreed.

I finished reading God's message to me—all twenty-two pages of it—and I made sure to not make any changes to the text. So I knew I would definitely get it back the next day.

The following morning when my alarm went off, the first thing I thought of was the message from God disguised as a patent. I couldn't wait for breakfast to be over so I could go to work. As soon as I got to work I went up to the corrections officer to receive my patents for the day.

The patent was not there.

And the officer had no memory of it.

It was as though it never existed.

I never got it back.

It—Really—Was—GOD!

The One who rescued me from addiction and darkness saw my great grief. And He loved me so much that when I was cut off from society, living in a razor-wire-enclosed cage, He gave me what can only be described as a miraculous message. He supernaturally and miraculously met me in the exact place of my need in order to speak to and comfort me!

And you too can count on Him to meet you at your exact place of need.

Chapter 10

ANGELS AT THE HALFWAY HOUSE

MY RELEASE DATE was only two weeks away when the officer came to escort me to what we inmates called *the clothing closet*. This is a room where inmates go to choose one outfit to wear on their release day if they don't have any family to send them clothing.

I watched for months as inmates' families mailed them clothing, usually with designer labels. (I was, after all, in a federal prison where many of the inmates had money.) I silently admired their outfits and wondered if FMC Carswell would let me keep one of my khaki prison pants and matching tops. Khaki was better than nothing! I would've been glad to have it.

The kind, spunky female officer ushered me into a large room that probably measured about fifteen feet square. Clothing in all colors and sizes hung from a rod that ran around the perimeter of the room.

"What size am I now?" I wondered.

I tried on outfit after outfit. Nothing looked right. They were not stylish. Finally, though, I settled on a pair of black pants and a large purple sweater that went down to my knees. I weighed 112 pounds, and the sweater was a size 1x, but I felt safe in it. I wanted to be invisible. I didn't want to wear anything tight or flashy.

The old Julie-before-Jesus used to wear provocative, revealing clothing, but the new Julie longed to be modest and unnoticed. The officer laughed and told me in no uncertain terms that she was *not* going to allow me to wear that baggy outfit. After ten minutes of arguing and pleading my case, she won. Reluctantly I chose another shirt, not as big as the purple sweater, but still baggy enough for me to feel safe.

On my release date (November 20, 2002) I was taken outside to a van. I was thirty-seven years old. I carried a single brown cardboard box with my inmate number written on it with a bold black Sharpie marker. Inside the box was everything I had left in the world—a few photos, a stack of cards from my mom, my court papers, and my plush, white terry bathrobe.

I got into the van that was to transport me out of the prison, and not long after that, the driver was pulling the van up to one of the terminals at the Dallas/Fort Worth airport and unceremoniously dropping me off on the sidewalk in front of the terminal.

As I walked toward the door of the terminal I felt like I had a neon sign on my forehead that flashed, "I WAS JUST RELEASED FROM FEDERAL PRISON."

I was free!

MY NEXT HOME

Since I was technically homeless and had no place to live, the Federal Bureau of Prisons guidelines mandated that I be sent back to San Diego—the city of my crime. So I had no choice but to return to the West Coast.

I checked in my cardboard box with the luggage attendant and proceeded to walk through the airport terminal to my gate. As I walked, I clutched my Bible to my chest and repeated out loud—over and over—*"Therefore, if anyone is in Christ,* [she] *is a new creation. The old has passed away, behold, the new has come"* (2 Corinthians 5:17 ESV).

There were no Bluetooth headsets yet, so people probably thought I was a crazy lady talking to myself, but I didn't care. I was so nervous. Throughout my incarceration I heard stories of women who gave their lives to Jesus in prison only to return to their old ways, habits, addictions, and lives of crime upon release.

"That is NOT going to be ME!" I determined.

My flight made it into San Diego, and I took a taxi to my final destination. I still remember the taxi driver's face as he pulled up in front of the old warehouse-turned-halfway-house in Barrio Logan—a seedy, shady, drug-infested, gang-inhabited area of San Diego. The two-story, solid concrete building was non-descript, and it sat in the middle of an old parking lot enclosed by a chain link fence.

"What are you doing HERE?" he asked with an undeniable fear in his voice.

"Oh, I'm just going to stay here for a little bit," I replied, embarrassed and not knowing what else to say.

The taxi driver jumped out, grabbed my cardboard box, threw it on the street next to me, and sped away. I stood in the middle of the street holding my cardboard box and staring at my new home.

Then a big smile erupted on my face!

I was out. I was F-R-E-E. I was living in San Diego. I would have a metal bunk bed to sleep in and free, prison-style smashed bologna sandwiches to eat. Praise the Lord!

Resolutely, I marched across the sidewalk to the door of the halfway house. When I knocked, I was met by an officer wearing a uniform and a gun. She told me to come in and sit down, and then she promptly left the room. When she returned, she had a small plastic cup in her hand. She then ushered me to a restroom, opened the door, and invited me inside.

I had to give her the dreaded urine sample.

Actually, I had become quite good at that procedure during my twenty-two months of incarceration, and I had gotten used to peeing in front of a complete stranger (always a woman officer).

She handed me the cup and waited. I had heard horror stories from women in prison that if you were unable to provide a urine sample within two hours of reaching the halfway house, then you would be *sent right back to prison*. I asked the officer if that was true. Without cracking a smile, she assured me it was.

Of all the times to get stage fright, that was *not* the time. But try as I did, I could not produce a drop. I tried everything. I turned on the water in the sink. I prayed out loud. The officer probably thought I was a lunatic. I literally cried out to Jesus to help me pee in that stupid cup!

The reality that I was going to go straight back to federal prison that day became more vivid with each passing minute. Finally, the officer told me to stretch my arm out and put my hand under the running water in the sink next to the toilet.

“Oh, thank you, God! Maybe she’s on my side after all,” I thought.

Finally, with only seven minutes to spare, I was able to fill the plastic cup with one inch of urine. Thankfully, the officer accepted my small offering and let me go to the office to check in with the guards.

Again God proved his faithfulness to me by putting the right people in my path at just the right time and in just the right place. It turned out that two of the guards, as well as my case manager, were Christians. That was so exciting to me, and bursting with the desire to share what God had done in my life, I gushed my Jesus-story to them.

I felt like I had a God-bubble around me, protecting and shielding me.

God placed Christians in my halfway house! I just knew He did that for me. Those amazing women encouraged me in my faith. They listened to all my Jesus-stories and tried hard not to smile too much, but it was difficult for them. I knew my joy was spilling out onto them, and they were a powerful source of joy and strength to me—another gift from God just as I was released from prison.

LOOKING FOR A JOB

I still remember meeting with my counselor. She explained that I had to get a job, but I showed her my prosthetic leg and told her that I really couldn't walk or stand all day long, because I dealt with neuropathy in my remaining foot. There was always the potential that I could get ulcers on that foot and face additional medical consequences. I further explained how Jesus had healed the ulcer in my foot after I gave my life to Him in prison.

She reiterated to me that I had to try to go to work, because that was the rule in the halfway house. If I didn't follow the rules, I would go back to prison—period.

I made up my mind to be the best rule-follower on the planet. I felt like every time I turned around, there were hoops to jump through, but for some odd reason, that delighted me. It was fun to follow the rules for the first time in my life! It was amazing that everything inside of me *wanted* to follow rules and be successful.

The Holy Spirit had surely made me a brand-new woman, and tears of joy came brimming up many times a day, causing me to run to one of my Christian *Angel Guards* and share my daily God-moments.

The next morning after my first meeting with my counselor, I woke up at 4:30 am to spend time with Jesus. I had spent nearly two years in federal prison practicing for that moment. I took a shower, dressed, and sat in the TV room, which was quiet in those early hours of the morning.

I read my Bible, wrote letters to God in my journal, and prayed before going downstairs for breakfast. I had to be out of the building by 8:00 am to look for a job. I picked up a brown paper-sack lunch at the guard station and headed for the trolley.

The San Diego trolley was an experience like no other. There was the blue line and the orange line. I often got on the wrong trolley and had to get off and wait for another one. My first day of job searching entailed walking for many city blocks and entering every store I came to in hopes that they were hiring ex-felons fresh out of prison.

I had no email address. I had no cell phone. And as soon as I told them I was staying at the halfway house, I was immediately turned away.

After a long day of walking around San Diego, I tried to find my way back to the trolley station. And much to my dismay, I was lost. I asked a few homeless people how to find the trolley and in the process gave away my sack lunch to someone who needed it more than I.

My foot was hurting, and I was in extreme pain by the time I returned to the halfway house. When I took off my shoes and socks, I saw it. There was a brand-new ulcer starting on my big toe. My shoes had been rubbing on it, but with my neuropathy, I didn't feel it, and I had walked on it all day long.

I wanted so badly to follow the rules of the halfway house set up by the Federal Bureau of Prisons. I really did want to get a job like a normal person. I wanted to earn my own paycheck. I felt my heart sink when I saw the ulcer on my toe. I knew I needed immediate medical treatment, but I had no insurance and no money.

I went to see my counselor to tell her what happened, but she explained there was no money for medical care for inmates. And she told me if I had a medical problem I would be sent back to prison. Then she told me there was a free clinic for homeless people a few blocks away and suggested I try going there in the morning to see if I could get help. That sounded like a much better option than going back to prison, so I gratefully agreed.

That night, I prayed fervently and asked the Lord to make a way for me to not go back to prison.

I had found a hallway upstairs in the halfway house with payphones hanging in it. No one was in the hallway, so I went up there, sat on the carpet, and cried and prayed for almost an hour. I told the Lord I really didn't want to go back to prison, but if somehow that was His will for me, then I would accept it. I promised God I would be the best witness for Jesus that I could possibly be even if I went back to prison. I promised God in that hallway that no matter where I was, in prison or out, I would serve Him with all my heart, mind, soul, and strength.

I woke up early the next morning to walk the three blocks to the clinic. My toe was bright red and swelling quickly; I knew it was already infected. I got to the clinic early and sat on the curb with all the other homeless people. As I checked in, the receptionist asked me for my home address. I told her I was staying at the halfway house down the street. She gave me a funny look, finished typing up my registration, handed me a piece of paper, and told me to sit down and wait.

As I sat in a chair, I unfolded the piece of paper. Under "Patient Name" it said *Julie Fitzpatrick*. Under "Address" it simply said, *homeless*.

A NEW RAY OF HOPE

I was living in a state of feeling blessed by God, and I didn't feel homeless. So it was a surreal feeling to look at that piece of paper and see the word "homeless" as my address.

I soon discovered, though, that being homeless with no money had its advantages. For I walked out of the clinic with antibiotic ointment, a bottle full of antibiotic tablets, and all the bandages I needed to last for a week. The doctor believed I would be okay!

The lieutenant at the halfway house gave me permission to stay home from job searching for the remainder of the week.

I was thankful, because I knew walking for eight hours a day looking for a job was not something I could endure.

As I was healing, I recalled a woman I met in the Texas prison. She told me she once worked for a government agency that pays for disabled people to go to college. Once again, the Lord provided a solution as I went to my counselor to ask if I could go to the local Department of Vocational Rehabilitation and inquire into the possibility they would pay for *me* to go to college.

I told her all about the promise I made to my mom—the promise that I was going to get my bachelor's degree and become a successful, productive member of society. My Christian counselor—an angel used by God in a season when I desperately needed one—gave me permission to go.

Two weeks and two appointments later, the Department of Vocational Rehabilitation accepted me as a client and agreed to pay for 100% of my college tuition, books, and supplies. The next step was securing permission from the lieutenant in charge at the halfway house. My counselor told me the lieutenant had never approved anyone living at the halfway house to go to college. The rule was, if you couldn't work full time, you must go back to prison.

I pled my case, explained my disability in detail, and assured my counselor that if I could go to college I would gain the skills and education necessary for me to get a job that took my disability into consideration. My counselor listened and said that she would go to the lieutenant on my behalf and ask for special permission. But she looked me in the eye and said, "Don't get your hopes up, because I don't know if he'll give permission for this."

I couldn't get the smile off my face; I was so full of excitement—so sure the Lord was going to work a miracle. I told her I would pray and just wait for her reply. I explained that I would go back to prison due to medical issues if I had to, but my preference would be to go to college and get a degree.

I was called back to my counselor's office the very next morning and informed that the lieutenant—who had never approved anything like that before—had just granted my request to go to college full time.

Hallelujah!

I was so excited, so full of joy, that I grabbed my counselor's arm and shook it while laughing. She started to crack a smile but quickly composed herself. She said, "Now Miss DeVere,[3] stop that! I have my job to do!"

But I could NOT stop smiling. I was so grateful! I was grateful for everything.

God was my way maker. He was my door opener. He was making a way where there was not supposed to be any way, and He was rolling out a red carpet for me to walk on toward my dreams because I was fully surrendered to Him.

All my hope was in Jesus. I was willing to walk through anything and accept every situation because I knew He would never let me down. And Paul's words to the believers in Rome, recorded in Romans chapter five, convinced me that Jesus would turn my *problems* into *purpose*. If I placed all my hope in Him, I'd NEVER be disappointed!

We can rejoice, too, when we run into problems and trials, for we know that they help us develop endurance. And

---

3 You see, even after my release from prison the employees of the Federal Bureau of Prisons insisted on using my middle name as part of my last name. That caused me a lot of grief, but I made it through that too.

endurance develops strength of character, and character strengthens our confident hope of salvation. And this hope will not lead to disappointment. For we know how dearly God loves us, because he has given us the Holy Spirit to fill our hearts with his love. (Romans 5:3-5)

FROM DREAM TO FULFILLMENT

It was pouring down rain the day I took the trolley to San Diego City College to register for school. I marched up the wide, steep concrete stairway that led to the admissions office in that cold, pelting rain while singing *Pomp and Circumstance* at the top of my lungs.

"Daaah dum ta dah duum dumm. Daaah dum ta dah dumm. Daaah dum ta dah duum dumm . . . "

The excitement of being on a college campus thrilled me from head to toe. I was actually doing it!

My mom was in the forefront of my thoughts and heart as I burst into the admissions office ready to register for college and start a new life looking like a drowned rat.

I shared Jesus with everyone, from the admissions staff to the career counselors to the bookstore clerk. Everywhere I went, I flashed a ridiculous smile and was quick and eager to share the reason why. I quickly learned that when you walk around with a huge smile on your face—as though you've just been given the best gift in the world—everyone wants to know what you are smiling about. You better believe I let them know!

I accepted demanding challenges head on. I ran *toward* everything that was difficult because I had spent a lifetime running *from* them. I was terrified of public speaking, so I signed up for an advanced public speaking course and volunteered to give my speech first when the time came to speak in front of the class.

And just the thought of microbiology made me nauseous, so I met with the professor and signed up to take it at an honors level. I knew I would not only have to process the information in the textbook but also share it with my classmates in a study group.

I passed public speaking with an "A"! And I passed microbiology with an "A"! Every time I stepped out in faith to accept the challenge of what looked impossible to conquer, the Lord went ahead of me and made a way. Following the advice of King David, I delighted in the Lord, and He was giving me the desires of my heart (Psalm 37:4).

I was learning, step by step, how to walk by faith and not by sight, and how to trust in the Lord with all my heart. In all that I did, I trusted God and sought His will. And He showed me moment by moment which path to take, which decision to make, what words to speak, and when to be quiet and not say a word.

The Apostle Paul told the Corinthians that,

> *God chose things the world considers foolish in order to shame those who think they are wise. And he chose things that are powerless to shame those who are powerful. God chose things despised by the world, things counted as nothing at all, and used them to bring to nothing what the world considers important.* (1 Corinthians 1:27-28)

Applying Paul's words to my life, God was proving that He was quite simply wanting to use *foolish little me*—who was deeply in love with him—to put to shame the wisdom of this world.

A perfect example presented itself when I was approached one day by my microbiology professor. He asked me to stay after class. I stayed behind as the other students left the room. He then said to me, "Julie, what's your story?"

"You're obviously an older student here at San Diego City College," He said. "And I see some of the younger students really look up to you. You influence everyone around you in a very positive way. And you are always so happy, so joyful. Can I hear the secret behind that?"

The Spirit of God filled the microbiology lab as I began to share my story with my professor. Emphasizing the great change that Jesus had made in me from the inside out, I gave him a nutshell version of my life story. My professor leaned closer as I spoke. My story was of great interest to him, but I didn't know why.

After I finished speaking, he sat back in his chair and took a deep breath.

I waited for a response from him during a long pause of silence.

Then he finally looked up at me and said, "Julie, I have been an atheist all my life. I don't believe in God. But my wife and my daughters are Christians. My wife has been trying to get me to go to church with her for years, and I have always told her no. But after hearing your story, I think I am going to go to church with her this Sunday."

THE MORAL OF THIS STORY

Reader, you MUST believe that your story matters! Your story matters deeply to God, because He wants to use your story to share his love, forgiveness, and life-transforming power with people who are lost, lonely, broken, and desperate.

God wants you to share your story with people who are lost and don't even realize it. He wants to use you wherever you are, wherever you work, and wherever you go. When you go to the store shopping, and wherever you go out to eat, God wants to use *your story* to touch the world.

And let's be clear. God does not need what you *don't* have in order to make a miracle out of your life. I *didn't* have a home. I was living in a halfway house. I *didn't* have any money. But God made a way for me to go to college. I *didn't* have fancy words or a strong background in theology. But God was using *simple me* to put to shame the lie of the enemy—the lie that had convinced a microbiology professor that evolution is true and Jesus doesn't exist.

God used me—a one-legged, ex-addict, ex-fugitive felon—to share the love and reality of Jesus with a doctorate-level science professor. All I did was share my story with my obvious love for God oozing from every pore in my body. And that was all it took for that educated man to entertain the possibility that God really IS.

AN UNEXPECTED ANSWER TO PRAYER

I would be a liar if I said that I gave my life to Jesus, got out of prison, and everything was perfect from that point on—no more pain, no more sorrow, no more struggling with guilt and shame—the end!

But that is definitely not my story.

I learned that life is hard. I learned that some people, even some family members, will never forgive you or forget your past.

But I also learned that walking in a living, daily relationship with Jesus Christ is the key to making it through every struggle and every rejection. That is the key to coming out of our struggles refined, strengthened, joyful, and whole.

Before I was released from prison I asked God to provide me with a car so I could get to medical appointments and go to college. The Lord graciously came through once again when my sister emailed me that she was sending our cousin over to the halfway house with a car—and not just any car, but a car of my very own!

I was beyond amazed. My sister purchased the car for me and asked my cousin to deliver it, and for that I am eternally grateful.

My cousin and his wife arrived at the halfway house with an almost new Hyundai—in perfect condition! My cousin barely spoke to me. He wouldn't look into my eyes. He was still very angry with me for who I used to be. He was angry with me for leaving my mom alone after the death of my father and running away to Mexico.

I didn't blame him for how he felt. I felt the same way about my horrible life choices. However, I had to live with myself and keep going. (Thank God for Jesus and His ever-present love and power to transform and save a wretched sinner like me.)

My cousin's wife went to the front desk of the halfway house to sign the required paperwork for dropping off my car and left me and my cousin sitting alone at a table. He still wouldn't look me in the face. I tried to swallow, but an enormous lump settled in my throat, and I had to fight back tears.

"I guess you're pretty mad at me for leaving mom and for everything I did that hurt my parents, aren't you?" I asked.

The words would barely come out.

Surely, he had to see the tears threatening to brim over my eyes and spill down my face. But without looking directly into my eyes, he nodded solemnly, and with disgust in his voice he told me, "I'm only here because my wife made me come. I do not want to be here."

His wife returned to the table and joined us. "Let me be clear," she said, "I am only here doing this for your mom and your sister. Otherwise, I would never have come. I am not doing this for you, I'm doing this for them."

That did it. There went the tears spilling over the shame that flushed my face.

I understood their view and their feelings. I had been a horrible drug addict who hurt our family through lies, theft, immorality, and more, for many years. I knew there would be people, even family, who would never want to believe in the *new* Julie, but that didn't lessen the pain of rejection.

I knew I would have to prove myself before I could regain their trust. And I was willing to spend however long it took and do the necessary work to rebuild my life with Jesus as the center, while hoping with all my heart that my family would eventually recognize and accept the change and come around in time.

Some of my family members did come around and welcome me into their lives once again. Others didn't. My cousin and his wife—the ones who dropped off the car at the halfway house—are among those who haven't forgiven me. And to this day, almost twenty years later as I write this book, they still haven't spoken to me.

Their open rejection of me the day they delivered the car to me hurt deeply at the time. I really wanted everyone to believe in the *changed Julie*, but God gave me an inner knowing that there would be those who couldn't bring themselves to believe in me. And God also gave me the grace and strength to accept it and keep moving forward into the exciting life to which He was calling me.

I fully accepted the fact that some people would never speak to me again, and I began trusting God with every part of my life, including every relationship, broken or restored.

Yes, it hurt to be rejected, but the constant, close love of my precious heavenly Father was greater than the pain of rejection. God gave me the grace to let go of things—including people and relationships—over which I had no control. And He gave me the grace and desire to follow Him wholeheartedly, day by day, moment by moment, and miracle by miracle!

MAKING IT THROUGH THE DAY

While in prison, I prayed and asked the Lord to provide me with a place to live, food to eat, clothes to wear, a college education, and transportation to get to all the places I needed to go in San Diego. Through God's provision of the car I further discovered God can and will provide our every need, and His provision will often come from the most unexpected places.

After receiving the car, since I had transportation of my own, the staff at the halfway house expected me to use it. I needed to go to Walmart for hygiene items. For the previous three months I had been taking the trolley everywhere I needed to go. And after not having driven a car in two years, I realized I was actually very nervous about driving.

I signed out and announced to the guard that I was going to Walmart. On the sign-out sheet I wrote "trolley" as my transportation. The guard caught on immediately and asked me why I was not taking my new car.

"I'm nervous. I haven't driven in two years! I don't want to drive yet. The trolley is safe," I told her.

"No, you are not taking the trolley. You have to drive your car," she informed me.

"Then will you come with me?" I pleaded. "Come with me! PLEASE. Come with me to Walmart. I don't want to drive alone. I'm nervous. Please come with me!"

The kind guard was struggling to remain strict and hide her smile. She stood firm, insisting that the only way I could go to Walmart was if I drove my car. She won the argument, and I got my keys and drove to Walmart—terrified—with my Bible on my lap, praying the whole way.

Driving felt so awkward at first. I wondered how it must feel for inmates getting out of prison after serving ten or twenty years when I was struggling to drive after serving less than two.

My trip to Walmart was a disaster. All I saw were families—happy families—and mommies with their children. I wondered if somehow my Tyler was in that Walmart with his new mommy. Every time I heard a child cry, or a little boy say something to his mom, I looked around to see if it could possibly be my Tyler.

I felt like I was losing my mind. The store and the people were closing in on me. The guilt and grief for my son rose up, once again, and threatened to choke me. The pain of not having Tyler anymore, and the reality of my failure as a mother, were unbearable.

The store was spinning, and the aisles full of home goods, makeup, candles, cards, and toys were all starting to blur. I couldn't focus on what I had come to purchase even though my list was short. I was there to buy shampoo, a brush, and deodorant, but I couldn't think clearly enough to locate those items.

I rushed blindly for the entrance doors and somehow made it to my car. I sat breathless in the driver's seat and gathered my thoughts. The tears began to flow as I wept and prayed.

"God, help me!" I pleaded. "God, this hurts so bad! Lord, I miss Tyler, and I know it was totally my fault that I lost him, but Daddy, my Abba, I can't go on like this. It's too painful! I can't even shop in a store without looking for Tyler. You've got to help me! I can't become a functioning member of society if I can't even find the shampoo aisle in a local Walmart. God, the pain is too much. Help me, Lord! Give me strength.

"Help me!"

As I prayed, I felt the presence of the Lord fill my car. He was with me. I made it back to the halfway house filled with the comfort and strength I needed to make it through that moment—through that day.

Chapter 11

WITNESSING TO THE BORDER PATROL

THE LORD KEPT leading me to His Word, and I read in Psalms that *"God places the lonely in families; he sets the prisoners free and gives them joy"* (Psalm 68:6a). I had no idea where I was going to live once my time at the halfway house ended, but I trusted God and looked forward to the time when I would once again not be so alone in my life.

I wanted the experience of being in a loving family once again, but I knew I needed to be very careful who I allowed into my circle of close friendships since I was a new Christian. So I prayed for guidance in that.

Even before my release from prison, I knew once I got out I needed to find a good church home so I could surround myself with people who really loved Jesus and who would influence my life in a positive way. I knew I was going to be released to live in the halfway house. So I wrote to two churches in San Diego from prison to ask if someone would be willing to pick me up from the halfway house and take me to church.

A female prison chaplain from one of the churches wrote me back. She promised to pick me up and take me to church as soon as the halfway house approved it, and I was so thrilled when she kept her promise.

I loved my Sundays with Chaplain Linda and her family. Until I got my car and started driving to church myself, she picked me up from the halfway house each Sunday and took me to her church, where I was accepted and loved by the members. They all knew I had just gotten out of prison, but they fully believed in the power of God to transform a repentant soul. They even asked me to speak and share my testimony at a special crusade called "Summer Sensation."

My probation officer was in attendance at the crusade and told me he had never had a client who showed such a dramatic life change.

One week before my release from the halfway house, I signed a contract to stay there for another six months because I had no other place to live. My Social Security disability was being reinstated, and I would be able to pay the halfway house one third of my check in exchange for the security of a roof over my head, a bed to sleep in, and food to eat.

I was doing incredibly well in my first semester at San Diego City College. And staying at the halfway house would allow me stability while I focused on my college degree. But my plans changed the next evening when Chaplain Linda stopped by the halfway house to visit me. We got to sit in the lobby, and she spoke to me while the guards—who were *very interested* in our conversation—listened in.

After sitting down, Chaplain Linda looked at me and said, "Julie, my husband and I have prayed, and we believe God wants you to come live with us."

My mouth dropped open, and my eyes widened in delight.

I found out my God was such a promise keeper! He was keeping His promise from Psalm 68:6.

"We will charge you $400 a month rent," she continued, "and you will be part of our family."

I glanced over at the guards and saw the disbelief on their faces.

Chaplain Linda gave her address and information to my caseworker. My new housing was approved by the Federal Bureau of Prisons the following day. I was excited, grateful, and terrified all at the same time.

I didn't want to disappoint God or Linda's family in any way. So I immediately went on a three day fast. I gave up food for those three days while praying that the Lord would make me a blessing to Chaplain Linda's family while I lived in their home.

I packed my bag and moved in with them three days later.

Shortly after moving in with Chaplain Linda and her family, I was asked if I wanted to join the church staff and put together the monthly church calendar. ME! On STAFF at a church! And believe it or not, I was also asked to help the pastors' wives count the tithe money.

Once, while counting money, it hit me. I looked up and shouted with joy, "HEY! Guess what? I've gone from counting drug money to counting God's money!"

I told the story of my high-speed drive to rescue the methamphetamine cooks from the Tijuana police with one hundred thousand dollars in my lap—trembling the whole way. We laughed and rejoiced over the goodness of God, and I was reminded of His words in Zephaniah.

At that time I will deal
with all who oppressed you.
I will rescue the lame;
I will gather the exiles.
I will give them praise and honor
in every land where they have suffered shame.
(Zephaniah 3:19 NIV)

BACK ACROSS THE BORDER

I joined the staff at my new church just in time for the annual staff retreat. Mama Linda told me that year they were going to take a cruise to Mexico—Baja California, Mexico! Rosarito Beach and Ensenada were the ports where the cruise ship was going to stop, and they wanted me to come on the cruise!

My federal probation orders stated that I was not to *enter the republic of Mexico*—period! And, if I did, I would immediately return to prison. I let Mama Linda know in no uncertain terms that I, Julie DeVere Fitzpatrick, ex-addict, felon-on-probation, would never, EVER, be allowed to go to Mexico on that cruise.

Unfazed, though, she kept telling me to just ask my probation officer if I could go. Finally, I decided to call him just to get her to stop telling me. To my absolute shock, he said yes!

But he not only said, yes, he also typed a letter for me to carry with me on the cruise so if I got stopped at the border, I could show the letter to the customs officers to prove I had official permission to be on that cruise and cross the very same international border I had crossed two years earlier with drugs.

It was settled. I was going on the staff cruise to Mexico.

It was the most incredible, surreal feeling to realize in expectation the magnitude of what that moment on the church cruise would represent. I would be cruising into the very same harbor where I had watched the cruise ships—lit up like Christmas trees—from the terrace of my rented beach house.

Then, I was a strung out, helpless, hopeless fugitive envying the happy people on those ships and longing to be one of them on board. It was unbelievable to think that on that trip I would be *on* one of those cruise ships—saved, clean, sober, living for Jesus and in relationship with Him, a college student doing well in school, and on staff at my church.

When the day arrived for us to board the Princess cruise ship, I was excited and nervous all at once. I made sure to pack my *God Journal*, where I wrote letters to the Lord each morning. My journal included letters, prayers, answers to prayer, and my favorite Scriptures that the Lord showed me, saying, "Julie, this promise is for you. I am going to bring this to pass in your life. So in faith, I need you to pray it and speak it out loud over your life while the promise is in progress."

I still have those journals after all these years, including the following entries of unforgettable God moments. Here are two actual excerpts from my *God Journal* while on the cruise:

> October 28, 2004
> 7:10 AM
>
> Dear Awesome Jesus,
>
> Here we are! I am on a cruise ship called "The Monarch of the Seas!" We are just off the shore of Ensenada, Mexico—at the VERY SAME PLACE where—four years earlier—I sat on the terrace of my rented beachfront

home at #18 Rancho Todos Santos and watched the cruise ships sail into the harbor.

I was a strung-out fugitive at that time. I had lost my left leg to amputation, my dad to lung cancer, and my only precious son, Tyler, had been taken from me because I was such a pathetic mess.

While I was grateful, at that time, for such a sight to behold—never did I dare think or even IMAGINE that four years later . . .

"I" would be the one coming in on a cruise ship . . .

clean and sober . . .

living for God . . .

a full-time college student . . .

with clear, precise goals . . .

on a staff retreat with a God-designated, "just for me" church!

What a PERFECT example of Ephesians 3:20 . . .

"Now to Him who is able to do IMMEASURABLY more than ALL we ask OR IMAGINE, according to His power that is at work within us."[4]

October 28, 2004

7:30 PM

Today I went shopping in downtown Ensenada with friends from church. One restaurant on a corner brought back especially poignant memories as I gazed at it, remembering the night I took my Mom (who was visiting me in Mexico) there for dinner.

4 From the New International Version of the Bible.

Even with multiple miraculous changes in my life, it is so painful to know I was an addict—a liar—who hurt my parents—but then I feel Jesus take me gently by my hand and say, "Come, my child, I have a work for you to do—My yoke is easy and My burden light—I love you—I will never leave you or forsake you—I know the plans I have for you, for good, not for evil, to give you a hope and a future."

And I cry . . .

"Jesus!!! But what about Tyler?"

And through my tears, Jesus reminds me of that moment in prison when I first cried out to Him about restoring my son. I was kneeling at my prison bunk, crying, with my head on my Bible, when the Holy Spirit nudged my heart, and I sat up and pushed my Bible open. My eyes fell immediately upon the open page, where Jeremiah 31:16-17 declared, *"Restrain your voice from weeping and your eyes from tears, for your work will be rewarded," declares the Lord. "They will return from the land of the enemy. So there is hope for your descendants," declares the Lord. "Your children will return to their own land"* [NIV].

I realize that in chapter thirty-one of Jeremiah, God was speaking through the prophet Jeremiah about the future restoration of Israel (His people). But in reading this passage, I discovered the compassionate heart of God, as a Father, to ransom and redeem all His children. And I knew that God (who is the same yesterday, today, and forever) was revealing both His heart and His character to me.

In doing so, He was teaching me that I could depend on Him—as my Father—to ransom and redeem my greatest mistakes, even by restoring my only son back into my life! And unwavering, I am STILL standing on all His promises!

STOPPED AT THE BORDER—AGAIN

The cruise was incredible. But it was time to return to San Diego. And I was stopped as soon as the U.S. customs agent ran my identification through their international system. I had pre-warned my church friends it would probably happen.

Suddenly, four very large and armed U.S. Marshals came and asked where my suitcases were. When I pointed to my suitcases, they picked them up and escorted me away from my group. I swallowed hard as I went with the officers. My palms were soaking wet with sweat. I was a nervous wreck, yet I determined to be brave and confident in who I was in Christ—a new creation.

I was taken by the marshals into a small room, and they locked the door behind them. Their demeanor was serious, and I could tell they thought they'd made a very important capture. They drilled me with questions, one after another.

"Where are you coming from?"

"Who are you traveling with?"

"Oh! A *church* group, huh?"

"Do you have any weapons on you?"

"Do you have any drugs?"

And then, the big question, "Have you ever been arrested before?"

The officer who asked if I had ever been arrested before was standing in front of a computer, looking down at the screen and then back up at me. I knew he had my criminal charges pulled up—Importation of Methamphetamine—the United States of America vs. Julie Devere Fitzpatrick!

I was trembling and scared, but I felt the Holy Spirit close to me as I heard my voice speak out with bold confidence.

"YES!" I told the officers. "I have been arrested before. I was arrested at this very Mexico/San Ysidro border on January 8, 2001, with four pounds of crystal methamphetamine duct taped around my waist. I had been addicted to alcohol and meth for seventeen years of my life, and I was a total mess. I just served twenty-two months in federal prison, and now I'm out on probation. I gave my life to Jesus Christ when I was in prison, and He changed everything about me."

The room was dead silent.

"With a church? You're here with a church group?" They were not quite believing me yet.

"Yes, I am! I exclaimed. "And if you walk outside, you will see the huge church bus with about thirty-five people waiting for me right now. I go to college, and I'm getting straight A's. Everything about my life has been transformed because of Jesus, and I even have permission to be here on this trip."

"Who gave you permission?" One of the officers shot out.

"My probation officer, Terry Marco," I announced confidently. "I have a letter that he wrote for me saying that I could be here on this trip."

"Where's the letter?" they demanded. I could tell they thought they finally had me.

"It's inside of my suitcase trapped inside your x-ray machine over there," I replied.

One of the officers got my suitcase, and I told him exactly where to find the letter as he unzipped my bag and started to search. The letter was right on top. He read it and took it to the U.S. Marshal who was in charge.

The head marshal took the letter. He read it carefully, and he slowly looked up at me, studying my eyes for the first time, and he asked, "Julie, did God really change you? Does that Jesus thing really work?"

"Yes! Oh, absolutely, YES!" I assured him.

I literally felt the atmosphere shift as a wall of invisible hostility came down. Suddenly the officers were smiling; then they started laughing.

The head officer looked at me and said something I will never forget. "My son is in prison for the same thing as you. He's a drug smuggler. He got caught smuggling drugs."

I could see the pain all over his face, and in that moment he simply looked like a dad—a very despondent dad who was looking for real hope that his son might still have a chance to change.

"My son calls me once a week. He is telling me he's going to church in prison and that he gave his life to Jesus. Is there really hope for him? Will this Jesus thing really help him?"

"Well, sir," I said, "if your son really gave his life to Jesus, God can change him. He can *absolutely* change him!

The U.S. Marshal was clearly touched with emotion, and all doubt that my story and my Jesus were real disappeared!

I was escorted out of the room, and that time with honor, by one of the officers who insisted on carrying my bags for me. As we stepped outside of the customs building into the sunshine, there sat the massive, shiny church bus with the name of the church painted on the side in huge letters.

My pastor and all the staff started cheering and clapping as I walked toward them grinning from ear to ear!

THE EARLY TERMINATION

In the midst of the miracles that were happening in my life, I suddenly remembered a very important promise that I had made to the federal judge who handed me my miraculously light sentence. Without his willingness to take a chance on me, I still would've been in prison.

Judge Miller's mercy in the courtroom on my sentencing day helped to open the door to every wonderful thing that was happening in my life. And that day he made a point to emphasize his request that I keep in touch with him and update him on my progress. As I thought on that, I decided then was a perfect time to let him know how well things were going. So I determined not to be one of the *nine lepers* who neglected to thank his benefactor.

I picked up my phone and called the Federal Defenders of San Diego. Sherree Brown, my federal defender, could tell me what I needed to do in order to report to Judge Miller, share my miracle stories with him, and thank him for my second chance at life.

"Julie, you can't just walk into a courtroom and talk to a federal judge," Sherree explained. "It's a security issue! The only way you will be able to get into Judge Miller's courtroom is if you have a legal reason to enter the courthouse."

I persisted in telling Sherree how important it was to me, and I asked her if there was some sort of legal motion I could file as an excuse to get into the courtroom.

After thinking for a moment, she said, "Well, Julie, you could file an Early Termination of Probation petition. You've been on probation for 18 months, which is not a very long time. Your motion may not be granted, but you're getting straight A's in school, and you are doing so well. It's worth a try. And it will get you in front of Judge Miller so you can update him on your life."

I agreed—ecstatically!

The wheels were set in motion.

I was assigned to a special attorney, Holly Sanderson, who agreed to handle my petition. In the "Statement of Facts," Holly wrote:

> Since her release, Ms. Fitzpatrick has excelled on supervised release. Most notably, Ms. Fitzpatrick has enrolled in college to get her bachelor's degree in the Health Sciences. She currently has a 4.0 grade point average and is a member of Phi Beta Kappa. In addition to her success in the area of education, Ms. Fitzpatrick is very involved in her church. She is involved in the choir (both performing and assisting with the children's choir), and she assists with the church calendar.

My court day arrived on December 10, 2004. I walked back into the same federal courtroom where almost four years earlier I had stood for my arraignment, shamefully strung out, in a wrinkled khaki prison uniform. But that day I wore a professional black skirt and matching blazer.

Attached to my motion for early termination of probation were my college transcripts and letters of recommendation from my pastor and several of my college professors. In addition, I had attached a personal letter updating Judge Miller on my life and thanking him profusely for my second chance.

The courtroom was packed full of inmates with shackles and handcuffs, prosecuting attorneys, federal defenders, court reporters, and probation officers. The buzz of multiple conversations happening at once was almost overwhelming. Suddenly, I heard my name called.

My moment had arrived to stand in front of Judge Miller and thank him in person for all he had done for me! The noise in the room lowered a bit, but people were still talking in hushed tones.

Judge Miller began to speak. "Ms. Fitzpatrick, I have read the evidence, and I am going to grant your motion for early termination of probation. But I want to hear from you right now. I have been waiting for this moment, and I want to talk to you and hear how you are doing."

I stepped forward, both nervous and excited at the same time as I began to speak. I told Judge Miller all that God was doing in my life and how Jesus had changed everything about me and made me a new person. A hush came over the courtroom, and I could have heard a pin drop. Everyone was then staring at me and listening to my story.

My prosecuting attorney was in the courtroom, along with my probation officer, and I eventually learned that both were there in favor of my early release from probation! Then, Judge Miller began to speak.

"You have certainly renewed my faith!" he exclaimed. "And judges *need* to hear these stories once in a while. I will always remember you, Ms. Fitzpatrick. I will keep your letter, and I will read it again from time to time. I am greatly touched by your letter and the successful direction in your life. Your success will guide me in the future when my intuition suggests that the person standing before me may be another Julie DeVere Fitzpatrick! Keep up the wonderful life you are creating for yourself."

With deep and heartfelt gratitude, my memory was pointed back to the silhouette inside a circle of light that had appeared across from me in the holding cell located behind that same courtroom. I had been warned by U.S. Marshals that I was facing the toughest judge in San Diego, and he was going to lock me up and throw away the key. Instead, back then that judge unlocked the door to my second chance at life, and now he was releasing me from probation early with honor and praise!

I was on cloud nine as my attorney and I walked out of the courtroom. My probation officer and the prosecuting attorney joined us in the elevator for the ride down to the ground floor of the courthouse. "You spoke with such eloquence," my probation officer told me. "We're very proud of you. You should be very proud of yourself."

Another God-miracle took place that day, and I got to give God ALL the glory. My heart is bursting even now thinking about it.

I, Julie Fitzpatrick, was walking with courage and faith, and I was learning with every step that nothing—*NOTHING*—is impossible with God!

Chapter 12

JULIE, PRAY FOR THIS MAN

THERE WERE TIMES back then when I couldn't afford a tube of toothpaste. I stood in front of the bathroom mirror holding my toothbrush in one hand and a flattened tube of toothpaste in the other. I looked in the mirror and said,

"Lord! I know this tube is flat and empty, but I also know you are Jehovah Jireh, the One who provides. I read in Genesis chapter twenty-two how you provided a ram in the thicket so Abraham didn't have to go through with sacrificing his son, Isaac. And in Second Corinthians we're told to walk by faith and not by sight, You are that same loving, providing God today! So Father, I'm asking you to please make toothpaste come out of this tube so I can brush my teeth."

At the end of my prayer I squeezed my toothpaste tube as hard as I could, and one glob of toothpaste came out of the tube—just enough to brush my teeth one time. Sometimes my totally flat tube of toothpaste miraculously kept providing globs of toothpaste—one glob at a time—for an entire two weeks until I could buy another tube. My God came through EVERY SINGLE TIME, and I never went a day without brushing my teeth after every meal.

I was getting straight A's in every class, and soon scholarship award letters began arriving in the mail. I interviewed with a number of benefactors (the people who provided the scholarships), and I was chosen as the recipient of six out of the eight scholarships I applied for. I was then invited to attend a scholarship awards banquet, and the benefactors were all there to hand each recipient a beautiful certificate and a check.

I could hardly contain my joy! I had shared my testimony with each and every benefactor, and they were so kind, so encouraging, and so proud of me for turning my life around and going to college. I was always quick to give Jesus the credit.

By the grace and the help of God, I maintained my 4.0 GPA and was given great favor on that campus.

Then I learned about another very prestigious scholarship—the most prestigious one. It was the Chancellor's Award, and it only went to a student who had a perfect 4.0 all the way through his or her degree program.

Normally, the Chancellor's Award winner was always one of the graduates, and I still had one year remaining to get my Associate of Arts degree. But the essay topic for the award was "Describe how you have overcome adversity to become a 4.0 student at City College." So I couldn't resist and applied for it!

There were a number of truly incredible applicants going out for that award, and I didn't expect to win. But since my professors also strongly encouraged me to apply, I did. I was interviewed by two separate committees and the Chancellor herself, and I put the results in God's hands.

My hands started trembling when the letter arrived in the mail from the scholarship committee. I opened it and read the beginning of the first sentence. Its first words were simply,

"Congratulations! You have been chosen . . .," and I started screaming with joy!

Mama Linda and her husband, Antonio, were so proud of me. I immediately called a few long-lost family members with whom I had very recently reconnected over the previous couple of years—including my Uncle Bob, my cousin Sue, and her husband, Jeff—and they jubilantly shared their excitement over my success.

Then, believe it or not, Constance Carroll, the Chancellor, insisted that I be the student speaker for that year's graduation ceremonies even though I was not graduating until the following year.

One of my favorite life verses, Zephaniah 3:19, says in part, "*I will give them praise and honor in every land where they have suffered shame*" (NIV). I suffered the shameful consequences of my own poor life choices when I went to federal prison in San Diego in 2001. And in 2005—only four years later—I was the student who stood on the stage at the Spreckels Organ Pavilion in Balboa Park,[5] San Diego, with top honors!

In my speech I shared a brief snippet of my story, and I told the graduating class of 2005 to never, ever give up! I was even written up in the local newspaper with the heading, *San Diego City College Student Overcomes Adversity*.

Psalm 27:13 declares, "*I remain confident of this: I will see the goodness of the LORD in the land of the living*" (NIV). I was literally living this out! Even as I am writing this book you have in your hand, I am at a loss for words to adequately describe the depth and reality of the joy that comes from seeing and experiencing God's Word when it comes to life.

---

5 https://balboapark.org/arts-culture/spreckels-organ-pavilion/

And still to this day, nearly twenty years later, I am walking in the goodness of His promises.

God also wants to give you your own story that testifies to His power and miraculous work in transforming your life. And that is the reason—*you* are the reason—God had me write this book.

Yes—*YOU*!

God took me from a life of shame to a life of significance. If shame is your reality today, surrender it to God with all your circumstances, all your heart, and all your life. Be *patient* while He goes to work on your behalf. Do your part and trust God to *be* God and do *His* part! Trust *God's* ways and *His* timing. Keep your mind ever focused on the goals He has set before you.

You will never regret it!

PRAYING FOR THE IMPOSSIBLE

The thought of being a wife and having my own Christian husband would flash through my mind on rare occasions, but each time it did, I immediately rejected it! I was forty years old, and I had been out of prison for a little over two years. I loved my new life and my adventures with Jesus. After all the pain, anguish, abuse, and toxicity I'd been through, I decided it was just going to be "Jesus and me" forever.

Yet somewhere in the deep recesses of my mind, I didn't want to remain the forty-year-old woman renting a bedroom in someone else's home. So I began to consider once again what it might be like to realize the white-picket-fence dream with my very own home and my very own husband.

One day during my morning prayer time, when nobody else was home and I was on my knees praying for different friends and situations, a hush came over me, and I became very still. Timidly, almost like a little child, I came before the Lord.

"God, I'm starting to think that I'd really like my own . . . husband . . . again one day. But God, I want him to be a strong Christian. And I want him to be on fire for you and to be in church every time the doors are open. And GOD! . . . "

I was starting to get very brave.

" . . . I want him to be tall! And I want him to have a great sense of humor."

Boldly, I was giving God a list of *must haves.*

"And Lord! I want him to love me," I said as my voice began to taper off, "with all his heart."

Oh! The realization of what I had just prayed hit me like a ton of bricks. Once he learned about my life story and my background, no man would love me with all his heart. I had just asked God to do something for me that was not possible.

So like a small child who picks up a gift and has to put it down because it doesn't belong to her, I whispered, "Never mind, God; that's impossible."

Momentarily I felt saddened, alone, and unwanted as I got up off my knees and stood to my feet. Then I decided to shake it off. I had homework to do and worship songs to learn by Sunday morning (since I was in the choir at church).

I had a wonderful life with Jesus, and one day my Lord and Savior was going to restore my son to me. I believed that. So I was determined to stay focused on the goal—the dream, the desire of my heart—to once again be reunited with my son. Nothing was going to shake me from it.

Living in a rented bedroom in the home of a Christian family who loved Jesus was a blessing beyond description to me, and I was determined that if I never had my own home or husband, I would still do my best to thrive in my second chance at life and become a mother my son would be proud to find one day.

THE REQUEST

About two weeks after I prayed the impossible prayer, I got a phone call from one of my friends. Theresa was the Children's Pastor at a church in Temecula that had been planted by Mama Linda's daughter, Jessie, and her husband, Rick.

Since I sang faithfully in my church choir and served on the worship team in San Diego, we called every Sunday after church, excited to swap God stories and tell each other all about what happened in our services that week. We both loved Jesus with all our hearts and enjoyed sharing our experiences.

On that Sunday, Theresa began the conversation fervently with, "Julie! Pray for this man!"

"It's so sad," she said. "He visited our church for the first time today and sat in the back row, and he cried the whole time." I could tell from her voice that she was completely heartbroken.

"Okay," I responded, "I'll pray for him. What happened?"

"His wife died!"

"Oh NO! What's his name?" I asked.

"I don't know his name," Theresa explained. "He left as soon as church ended, and I didn't get to talk to him. A few of the men in our church ran after and caught him on the sidewalk on his way to his car. They hugged him and told him to come back, but I don't know if he will or not."

"That's okay," I reassured her. "God knows his name."

I understood the grief that comes with the loss of someone close. Although I had never experienced the death of a spouse, the pain of losing my parents was still very acute, and I felt a deep empathy and compassion for that man I'd never met.

I began to pray daily for him with all my heart. I asked the Lord to heal his broken heart and help him and his family during their grieving process. I had a strong sense that the Lord was moving in response to my believing prayers for him. And I believed he was experiencing God's comfort, peace, and strength in what had to be his darkest hour.

I soon learned the man's name was Mike. And I cried tears of joy when Theresa told me Mike returned to church the following weekend and went to the altar at the end of the service to recommit his life to Jesus Christ!

"Wow, God!" I thought as she told me. "You must have heard my prayers for him!"

Theresa and I rejoiced together at the power of God at work in Mike's life and all the other people on our prayer list.

THAT MAN OVER THERE

A few months later, I drove to Temecula to spend a "girls' weekend" with Theresa, and I went to church with her on Sunday morning. As soon as I walked into the lobby of the church, I saw a tall military man holding an adorable baby in a car seat. I gushed over the baby, got her to smile at me, and went into the sanctuary to find a seat.

Before I could sit down, a young woman whom I barely knew marched over to me and said, "Do you see that man over there?" She was pointing at that same man with the baby.

"Yes," I responded.

"That's your future husband!" she said. And then she promptly turned and walked away.

I felt a flush of embarrassment as I hoped he hadn't noticed the woman pointing at him. I quickly looked away and hurriedly found a seat. I learned later the man with the baby was Mike, and the baby was his new granddaughter.

As I sat there waiting for church to start, I couldn't help wondering if the Lord had orchestrated the woman's revelation. "She doesn't know me, so how could she say that?" I wondered. "God, could that really be true? Did You speak to her, Lord, and have her come tell me that?"

I met Theresa and a group of our church friends several months later at a conference called *Deeper Life*. I missed Tyler terribly, and I went to Deeper Life seeking a personal, powerful encounter with God. Mike was also there, and I learned later that he had come seeking healing from his deep grief over the loss of his wife of twenty years.

At the end of the conference, I responded to the altar call and stayed on my knees for about 45 minutes, weeping and crying out to God for comfort and strength. Finally, it seemed as though God wasn't going to answer me. I felt nothing spiritual happening, and I didn't sense any message from the Lord.

Disappointed, I stood to my feet and was about to leave when one of the pastors who was praying over the people at the altar stopped right in front of me and stared deeply into my eyes. He reached out and put his hand on my head and he began to prophesy, "Be patient with God. He's been patient with you! Your miracle is coming!"

"It's TYLER!" I thought as the pastor prayed for me. "Tyler is coming!"

But as the pastor continued praying I saw a man's face. And it was not just any man. The face I kept seeing was . . . MIKE!

I quickly shook my head and thought, "No, God, it's Tyler! My miracle is NOT a man. My miracle is TYLER!"

But yet again I saw Mike's face in the vision God was giving me.

CHRISTMAS EVE SCARE TACTICS

Not long after the Deeper Life Conference, I got a phone call from Deidra, a pastor's wife who served on staff at the Temecula church.

"Julie, I want to invite you to come for dinner at our home on Christmas Eve. Are you busy? Do you have plans?" she asked. "Mike is going to be there. You need to come."

"Oh dear," I thought. "Lord, I know I prayed for a husband, but then I changed my mind. Remember, Lord? Because once somebody knows about my past, he won't want me. Nobody will be able or willing to love me with all his heart."

With all those anxious thoughts running rampant through my mind, I grew quiet. Deidra kept insisting that I come spend Christmas Eve with her family and Mike, and finally, I reluctantly agreed.

Deep inside I became acutely aware of the fact that I had no real relationship skills. All of my previous relationships had been overwhelming failures, full of physical and emotional abuse, substance use, volatile arguments, and despondently lonely tears. I had become an effective communicator and a compassionate, loving, joy-filled woman, but my past relationships that had crushed my spirit still had an effect on my confidence and trust in men.

I had never been treated with authentic love, value, or respect, so I had never been without pain in those disastrous relationships. And I had responded to that with anger, screaming, throwing things, and finally, substance abuse to numb the pain. I still had zero communication skills when it came to having a relationship with a man.

By the time Christmas Eve arrived, I deeply regretted accepting Deidra's invitation. I was so nervous! "What was I thinking when I agreed to this?" I told myself over and over. But still, even with that, the dream of having my own home and my own husband continued to play across my mind and stir my excitement as I went to great pains getting ready for the evening.

I worked hard on curling my waist-long, brown hair instead of tying it up in a bun on top of my head, and I carefully selected a chocolate-brown lace skirt, a cream-white lace blouse for an elegant contrast, and a brown fitted jacket with matching brown leather boots. I took one last approving look in the mirror and left the house with conflicting emotions.

The part of me that longed for the white picket fence dream was excited, but the honest, realistic part of me was terrified that I didn't have what it took to make the dream come true.

I arrived at Deidre's house on time and slowly, hesitantly, walked to her front door. When I knocked, Deidra and her family welcomed me warmly. She graciously accepted the gourmet pumpkin cheesecake I had purchased from The Cheesecake Factory, and she told me to follow her into the kitchen.

"Mike isn't here yet," I thought. "There's STILL TIME TO RUN!"

It's strange how the ghosts of old habits reappear at the most unexpected times.

"Listen," Deidra said as if she could read my thoughts. "This is God! You two are meant to be together. Mike needs you, but he just doesn't know it yet."

"Did you tell him I just got out of prison?" I asked. "Does he know my testimony?"

"He doesn't need to know," Dee insisted with assurance in her voice. "It doesn't matter."

"Uh oh. He needs to KNOW these things!" I stated quite emphatically.

Everything in me wanted to make up an excuse and leave, but instead, the new Julie remained, sitting nervously at Dee's kitchen island, chatting with her while she finished working on dinner until there was a knock at the front door.

I froze as Mike walked in carrying a huge platter of shrimp from Costco. He stopped when he saw me, tilted his head, and smiled.

"Oh no!" I thought. "I know I've seen this man several times before, but, gosh, he really IS a tall, good looking man with charisma!" My mind was spinning.

"I've got to scare him away, because he will never be interested once he hears my story. Wait! That's it! All I have to do is tell him my story, and that will surely make him run the other way."

I waited until we were all sitting down at the table eating Deidra's delicious dinner. Mike politely said, "So, you're in college?"

I put down my fork and smiled brilliantly at him. I knew I had to let the cat out of the bag, and soon!

"Yes, I'm working on my associate's degree at San Diego City College, and then I'm going to start my bachelor's degree."

"You must be very smart!" Mike said.

It was time! I HAD to tell him the truth.

"You DO know that I was addicted to alcohol and drugs for seventeen years, right?"

"Ummm, no. I didn't know that."

"Yep. And you DO know I just got out of federal prison, right?"

"No, I didn't know that either," Mike said.

Strangely, he didn't look deterred by my confession. He was staring straight into my eyes, smiling, totally unfazed by what I was telling him. Deidra and her family were chuckling, and it was becoming quite comical—at least to them. I had one more weapon in my back pocket. And that one was sure to scare him away.

"You DO know that I only have ONE leg, right?

"What? You have TWO legs! What are you talking about? I saw you at the altar praying at Deeper Life. You have two legs!"

Mike looked confused, and everyone else began laughing uproariously. They knew I was trying to scare Mike off because I was trying to protect myself from eventual rejection. But they also knew Mike was not going to reject me and God was the One bringing us together.

"Nope!" I announced. "One is a prosthetic!"

I then lifted the hem of my skirt and showed Mike my below-the-knee prosthesis.

"Oh! WOW! I couldn't even tell you had a prosthesis!" Mike exclaimed.

I then said, "You can leave now if you want to."

I was eager to let him know he was off the hook and free to not consider pursuing a relationship with me.

"What are you talking about? I haven't had dessert yet!"

Then Mike winked at me, smiled, and said, "I'm not going ANYWHERE!"

Chapter 13

MIKE'S STORY

TRUE TO HIS word on that unforgettable Christmas Eve, Mike didn't go anywhere. He emailed me a few days later, still amused by my scare tactics. We fell in love quickly and spent hours on the phone every evening talking about the Lord and getting to know one another as we took turns sharing our life stories.

I could hardly contain my excitement whenever Mike drove from Temecula to San Diego to take me out for dinner or coffee. And I quickly learned that Mike, too, had a testimony. It was heartbreaking yet beautiful at the same time.

Mike grew up in rural central Florida, and his life growing up in a trailer park was not easy. Mike revealed to me that life for him was "really hard." Fortunately, there were special times Mike remembered during his youth that helped him get through those difficult years.

The Church of God in La Belle, Florida, had a ministry that sent out a bus to pick up young people who didn't have a way to get to Sunday services. Mike's parents allowed him to be picked up in the morning for church and brought back home in the afternoon. Mike shared with me that even as a small child he felt a longing to know the Lord, and he described it as having a "huge soft spot" in the center of his heart when it came to God!

Mike attended Sunday school and was soon baptized, but he didn't really understand the depth of what that meant. Later, when he was seventeen, Mike responded to an altar call, repented of his sins, and earnestly asked Jesus Christ to be the Lord of his life. He even received the baptism of the Holy Spirit in that little Church of God that day. But he had no clue as to what he should do next.

Just as he did on other Sundays, Mike left the church service and rode the bus back home. And it was unfortunate that nobody in the church followed up and began mentoring him or teaching him how to build a personal relationship with God and live as a Christian.

After giving his life to the Lord, Mike decided he wanted to get as far away from the trailer park as possible, so one month after his salvation experience at church, he enlisted in the United States Navy and left Florida to start a new life.

Life as a sailor was not the ideal setting for a brand-new Christian. For the first time in his life, Mike was out on his own traveling all over the world. Exotic ports, foreign women, and free-flowing alcohol all took precedence as he began to indulge in a lifestyle that was far from the one God had created for him.

Four years later, while stationed in Long Beach, Mike met a beautiful woman from the Philippines. Her name was Trina. She seemed so exotic to him, not like anyone he had ever met. After seeing each other for only a few months, Mike and Trina were married, but marriage was not something he was ready or prepared for.

He was used to his wild lifestyle and freedom. Mike admitted he was not always a good husband to Trina. He hung his head in shame as he hesitantly confided to me that he had serious anger issues from his childhood experiences, and he took that anger out on Trina.

In addition to dealing with alcohol and anger issues, Mike developed a gambling problem while he was stationed in Fallon, Nevada. His addiction so controlled Mike that even while Trina was in the hospital giving birth to their daughter, Susan, he was in a casino gambling away her paycheck. Shortly thereafter, though, Mike was transferred back to Long Beach and away from the temptation of the casinos, and that helped him control his gambling issues.

In all honesty, Mike loved his little family to the best of his ability considering that he was a broken man inside who had never known what a functional, healthy family life was all about.

Mike spent a fair share of his Navy years traveling and going overseas, missing many holidays with his wife and daughter. But in return for his faithful service to his country, Mike eventually made Chief, and then Senior Chief. Life seemed good until the summer of 1999, when after fourteen years of marriage Trina was diagnosed with stage 3B breast cancer.

Chemotherapy for Trina began immediately following her diagnosis. Stage 3B cancer is very advanced, and Mike said he was terrified that his wife was going to die. And united by a mixture of fear and love, He and Trina grew much closer during that time.

They cried together, and Mike took her to all of her medical appointments and bought her special health food to improve her chances of healing. He also spent hours scanning websites with breast cancer research in order to become well informed on the subject, and he joined online support groups for families of breast cancer victims. He, too, became a sideline victim of the dreaded disease.

Facing the possibility of losing Trina, all Mike could think about was his daughter, Susan. He wondered how he could possibly raise her alone. She was only thirteen years old.

Even though Mike was not living for God at the time, he became acutely aware of Him then! But he was also convinced he was unworthy to ask for anything from God, especially after turning his back on Him and living "his way" for so many years. He didn't want to seem greedy or ask for too much, so he prayed, "God, please don't take my wife. But if you have to take Trina, please don't take her until Susan graduates from high school."

Mike was in tears when he told me that even though he was not serving the Lord, God in His great and endless mercy *answered his prayer*. After one year of chemo, radiation, and a mastectomy, Trina was fine. There was no sign of cancer!

Trina was healed, and life seemed to go back to normal. However, just beneath the surface, a new journey was beginning. The Holy Spirit was gently seeking Mike and calling out to his heart.

While Mike carpooled to Camp Pendleton with a group of Christian men, they listened to Christian radio in the car. Mike's heart was being deeply touched by what he heard on the radio, and while sitting in the back seat, hot tears sometimes streamed silently down his face as he listened to the Word of God.

Then late in the summer of 2004, Mike heard a voice speaking to him—not an audible voice, but a very clear voice inside his head—saying, "Mike, you better get your family in church before it's too late."

He knew it was God speaking to him, but his flesh was fighting against it. As more time passed, Mike kept dragging his feet and procrastinating. He shared with me that back then he was too blind to see or understand that life as he knew it was about to be shaken to its very foundation. He was too distracted to realize that God was speaking to him, calling him for a purpose greater than anything he had ever experienced.

On January 14, 2005, Mike received a phone call at work. It was his daughter, Susan. "Hey, Mom's eyes are yellow," she said.

"What? You're crazy!" Mike exclaimed.

He reassured Susan that it must be the light hitting her Mom's eyes just right, and the light was making them appear yellow. Susan kept insisting though, "No, Dad, her eyes really are yellow!"

Mike left work, and sure enough, Trina's eyes were yellow, and so was her skin. He rushed her to the hospital where they learned Trina's cancer had returned and had metastasized. Microscopic bits of cancer were throughout all her organs. As Trina lay in a coma, Mike sat next to her overwhelmed by a mixture of shock and grief.

Then God spoke to him again in a quiet voice. "You better get what's left of your family in church before it's too late!"

A few days later, Mike's wife of twenty years was gone.

Trina's death left Mike completely broken. He felt as though he had fallen as low as any man could fall. He was lost, hurting, and desperate. And he realized where he needed to go.

On his daily commute to Camp Pendleton, Mike had seen a sign on the side of the 15 Freeway for a Pentecostal Church, and not long after the funeral, God led him directly to that church. Mike sat in the back row and cried despondently for the first three Sundays. All he could do was wonder why it was not him who had suffered and died.

"Why did it have to be Trina?"

All she had ever done was love him in spite of the way he hurt her by his actions and his uncaring words. It was too late to tell her how very sorry he was for the way he had treated her for most of the twenty years of their marriage.

Grief for the loss of someone dear shatters the heart, but grief mixed with regret shreds the soul.

After church, Mike used to drive to the cemetery and ask God to somehow tell Trina that he deeply regretted the way he had treated her. He was overwhelmed with grief over the man he had been, and he knew in his heart that he didn't ever want to be that man again.

Mike instinctively knew he was being given his last chance to return to God. He also knew his actions at that pivotal point in his life would have a lasting effect on his daughter. And it was at that crucial moment when he wholeheartedly repented of his sins and gave his life completely over to Jesus Christ.

In Mike's words, "I was home."

We read these words of David in Psalm chapter eighteen: *"He reached down from heaven and rescued me; he drew me out of deep waters . . .. He led me to a place of safety; he rescued me because he delights in me"* (Psalm 18:16-19). Mike was experiencing what David experienced long ago. God still does the same things today that He has always done for those who put their trust in Him.

And He will certainly do them for you!

I later learned that during the months when I was in San Diego praying for Mike and his daughter, before I ever met them, Mike was beginning to feel God's presence with him every waking moment as he clung to his Lord for comfort, strength, and peace.

During the first months after Trina died, Mike went for his daily four-mile run and then headed for the Chief's Mess to shower and change. But before he could put on his uniform, he often collapsed in a heap on the tile floor, curled up in the fetal position, and sobbed uncontrollably. It was during those moments when Mike felt the love of God as He wrapped His arms around Mike and said, "This will soon pass, my son. I have plans for you!"

Now Mike says it took two people to die in order to get his attention—his wife, and Jesus!

Our lives are composed of seasons, and only God knows how long those seasons will last. We read in Ecclesiastes, *"For everything there is a season, a time for every activity under heaven . . . a time to cry and a time to laugh, a time to grieve and a time to dance"* (Ecclesiastes 3:1-4).

Mike's time to grieve was coming to an end when he attended the Deeper Life Christian Conference in November of 2005. At the end of the evening, Mike went to the altar, got down on his knees, and poured out his heart to the Lord. Mike said he literally felt God purging him of every bit of grief in that moment. And with every tear he shed, another portion of grief was taken from him.

Mike's season of grief ended that evening. God took every bit of his pain away and turned his mourning into dancing just like He did for King David.

> *You have turned my mourning into joyful dancing. You have taken away my clothes of mourning and clothed me with joy.* (Psalm 30:11)

God is truly the God of restoration!

Chapter 14

LOOKING FOR TYLER

NEXT TO JESUS, Mike quickly became my best friend. I found him so easy to talk to, and I told him everything about my life. Mike never judged me, and he always believed in the miraculous change that God made in my life. He quickly opened his heart and life to me, and he frequently did things to bless me and make me feel special.

One Sunday he drove to San Diego to visit my church on a day when I was scheduled to sing a special solo worship song. He knew I was on Social Security disability as my only source of income, and so on that particular Sunday he snuck money into my Bible while I was up on the platform singing.

Later that evening he called me from home. "Julie, tell me again what your favorite verse in the Bible is."

"Jeremiah 29:11!" I exclaimed emphatically.

"Read it to me." Mike said.

"For I know the plans I have for you, declares the Lord . . . "

"No! Don't read it from memory! Open up your Bible and read it from your Bible!"

Unsuspecting, I grabbed my Bible and opened it to the book of Jeremiah to find my favorite verse. Out fell a stack of twenty-dollar bills! Mike had snuck eighty dollars into my Bible.

Overwhelmed by his generosity and thoughtfulness, I managed to thank Mike through my tears. Eighty dollars would fill my gas tank and get me back and forth to school and church for over a month!

Mike told me many times a day in phone calls and text messages that he was in love with me. I felt the same way toward him. It was almost surreal to think that someone could love ME, Julie, after learning my entire life story. But Mike *did* love me, and he *wanted* to become a part of my journey.

Mike didn't just love me; he also believed in me. He believed in the "new" Julie—the "changed" Julie! Further, he also knew the deepest desire of my heart was to see my son again, and he supported me in that.

"Where do you think Tyler is?" Mike asked me one time. "Do you have any idea? He needs to know you. He needs to know his mom."

"I know he is with his dad, somewhere in Orange County," I said, "but they moved, and I have no idea where they are now."

It didn't take Mike long to do an internet search and find out where Tyler and his dad were living. My intention was not to disrupt or interrupt Tyler's life. I had no idea how he was doing or how well he had adjusted to being abruptly taken from me and given to his dad.

I wanted to go to court and request visitation with my son. I was pretty sure that it would not be granted, but I at least wanted to try. I wanted Tyler to know that his mamma had gotten her life together and had at least tried to find him and see him.

Mike suggested that we drive down and sit in front of the house to see if it was the correct address before getting an attorney to file a request for visitation. I agreed, and so one morning Mike picked me up at 4:00 am, and we drove to the address he had found for Tyler's dad. It was very overcast and foggy that morning, and we sat silently in Mike's truck waiting to see who would come out of the house.

I was praying silently.

"Lord! You know my heart! All I want to do is know if this is where Tyler lives so I can ask a judge for visitation. And God, I just want to know if my son is okay—if he's happy. I'm okay with not being able to see him yet if that is how things go. I only want your perfect will, Father! Nothing different."

Five minutes later, Mike grabbed my arm and shook me.

"JULIE! LOOK! It's your son!"

I looked up to see . . . TYLER!

There he was!

After seven long years of not seeing my little boy or knowing where he was, he was *right in front of me.* I knew it was him!

With every fiber of my being, and with every instinct of a mother, I knew it was Tyler. He wore khaki shorts, a white polo style shirt, and a backpack ready to go to school. But what I really honed in on was the fact that he was walking slowly down the driveway with his head hanging down, looking at the ground, as though he were very sad.

My heart broke! Everything in me wanted to jump out of the truck and shout, "TYLER! TYLER! It's MOMMA!" Even while I knew instinctively that would be the wrong thing to do, my momma's heart yearned to hold my little boy.

Moments later, Tyler's dad came out of the house and walked to the car. He let Tyler in and drove off to take him to school.

Mike and I had our answer! That was where Tyler lived, and that would be the address I would send paperwork to when I filed a petition to ask for visitation with my son.

Mike started his truck and looked at me. "Are you okay?"

Tears were streaming down my face.

"I wanted to get out and run to him!" I sobbed.

"Well, that wouldn't be the right thing to do. You can't do that." Mike said softly, reaching out to hold my hand.

"Yes, I know," I agreed.

"Don't worry, Julie. I'll help you when you go to court. If you need money for an attorney, I'll help you. I'll pay for it.

"Julie! God let you see your son today!"

WHEN GOD SAYS "NOT YET"

True to his word, Mike helped me get an attorney to file a motion for visitation with Tyler.

I heard stories of children who were separated from a parent during bitter custody battles, and once they turned eighteen they started searching for the parents they had been separated from, even if their parents had failed them in some way. That helped me feel encouraged.

In my heart, though, I didn't want Tyler to come looking for me, discover I had completely changed, gotten clean and sober, and then hear him say, "Mamma, oh, Mamma! Why didn't you come looking for me? Wasn't I worth it? Why didn't you at least try to find me?" So I felt strongly that I needed to take the initiative right away.

If I went to court to ask a judge for visitation—even supervised visitation—even if Tyler was not yet ready to see me, at least he would know I *tried*. I had to try to see my son, and the right way to do that would not be to surprise him with a knock on the front door. I had to take the right steps and go through proper legal procedures.

My emotions were all over the place. I was fearful of having to go to court and face Tyler's dad. I had been put to great shame during the custody battle when the lifestyle I was living was brought out into the light of the courtroom in front of a judge, attorneys, and many of the people in the small southern town who came to watch my demise.

Yet I knew I was a totally changed woman—a new person just like 2 Corinthians 5:17 declares! So I pressed on.

As I prepared for dealing with another court action I remembered the moment when I was in federal prison and made up my mind to be courageous. I was still committed to that. And I knew I had literally been preparing myself mentally, emotionally, and spiritually for *that* moment! It was time to take action.

To arm myself for the battle that I knew was ahead of me, I sat down at my computer and typed specific Scriptures that God had been showing me for years—Scriptures that encouraged me to pray, and Scriptures I knew to stand on once that moment came. I needed those Bible verses in front of me every day!

I typed out each Scripture in large font and printed out each one on an 8½ x 11 sheet of white paper. I then taped all those papers onto the walls around the perimeter of my bedroom. Every day, just as I did when I had taped Scriptures around the perimeter of my prison bunk, I sat on my bed and scanned the perimeter of the room, reading and declaring each Scripture out loud.

Luke 21:14-15 told me not to worry about defending myself, because God would give me the right words at the right time. Isaiah 50:7-9 reassured me that because the Lord was my helper, I would not be disgraced or put to shame.

Isaiah 54:15-17 promised me that no weapon turned against me would prevail, and that was my heritage as a servant of God. Zachariah chapter ten showed me that God would restore me because He had compassion on me, and that my child, Tyler, would see it and be joyful!

I read and prayed those and many more Scriptures over myself daily, and as I did, my heart was encouraged and strengthened for the journey ahead.

However, my fears of having to be put on the stand in a courtroom and answer for all of the sin, wickedness, and failures of my previous life turned out to be unfounded. Since Tyler was already twelve years old, the judge ruled that he should have his own legal representation. Tyler would be the one to decide if he wanted to see me or not.

When the court date arrived, Mike took time off from his military command in Camp Pendleton to drive me to the courthouse, praying with me the entire way. My hands were sweating, and my knees were trembling as Mike and I rode the elevator to the fifth floor where the family law hearings were held.

Two weeks earlier I had gotten the privilege of sending Tyler's attorney, Barbara, an email with a letter attached. In that letter, I shared truthfully about my years of addiction, as well as my story of radical life transformation in federal prison.

Barbara had asked me to write my story, and she promised to read it to Tyler so he could learn more about his mother while making the very important decision of whether or not to allow me to see him.

I had a feeling Tyler was not ready to see me, but I felt a small measure of hope rise in my heart as I wrote the letter.

After Barbara delivered the letter to Tyler, she was there to meet us when we got off the elevator, and she motioned for us to follow her to a quieter part of the hallway so she could speak to us.

"Your son does not want to see you," she told me. "I read him your letter, but he still does not want to see you. He is traumatized by everything that happened in the past. I am recommending to the judge that there be no contact."

Even though I was not surprised, it didn't stop the physical wrenching I felt in my heart at that moment. It felt as though a knife was being thrust straight through the center of my chest cavity. Guilt, shame, and remorse over my past came rushing back like a powerful tsunami.

Mike put his arm around me to comfort me as through my tears I managed to thank Barbara for representing Tyler so well and doing what was in his best interest.

Barbara walked away to speak with the judge, and as she did, Mike took hold of my shoulders and looked me square in the eyes. "I have a word from God for you," he said. "God said to tell you to *'trust in the Lord with all your heart and lean not on your own understanding. In all your ways acknowledge Him, and He shall direct your paths'* " (Proverbs 3:5-6 NKJV).

"Trust God, Julie!" Mike continued. "We KNEW this was going to happen. Your son is not ready to see you yet. He's still young, and he still lives with his dad. He'll want to see you one day. The day will come. He's not eighteen yet. Just keep trusting God!"

Oh, how grateful I was for Mike and the word from God he gave me at the moment I needed it the most! I was relieved to not have to go through shame and embarrassment in the courtroom, but I was also gripped with unspeakable grief to have heard spoken aloud what I already knew in my heart—that my only son was traumatized over my past mistakes and grievous failure as a mother.

Although I could tell that day would set me back emotionally, I knew it would only be temporary, because I had determined years earlier to walk through that moment with courage. I also was determined to continue to pray for my son to be healed mentally and emotionally from all he had endured. I was going to trust God and keep moving forward!

Not getting to see Tyler didn't negate the miracle God planned for the future. And a Scripture God gave me when I was in prison was a huge encouragement to me.

> *But now this is what the Lord says:*
> *"Do not weep any longer,*
> *for I will reward you," says the Lord.*
> *"Your children will come back to you*
> *from the distant land of the enemy.*
> *There is hope for your future," says the Lord.*
> *"Your children will come again to their own land.*
>
> (Jeremiah 31:16-17)

I had already clung to this promise in Jeremiah for five years, and I was determined not to give up.

God's plan was different from mine, and looking back, it's clear to see that God's message to us through Isaiah is absolutely true. God's plan was higher and better. It really was.

> *"My thoughts are nothing like your thoughts," says the* L*ORD.*
> *"And my ways are far beyond anything you could imagine.*
> *For just as the heavens are higher than the earth,*
> *so my ways are higher than your ways*
> *and my thoughts higher than your thoughts."*
>
> (Isaiah 55:8-9)

The rejection and piercing reminder of my shameful past stung, but the goodness and mercy of God, and the joy of walking through life with Jesus was truly greater. That joy was carrying me through every challenge as I kept my eyes focused on the One who, one day, would turn it all around.

A FLORIDA WEDDING

My graduation from San Diego City College was an accomplishment I will never forget. We arrived five hours early because I was so excited. The chairs weren't even set up yet! But with sweat dripping off his head and rolling into his eyes, Mike waited patiently with me in the torturous 105-degree summer heat wave. And he didn't complain once!

I was selected for the honor of leading the entire student body to the stage while carrying the American flag. And when *Pomp and Circumstance* began to play in the outdoor pavilion, I marched with GREAT joy, holding the American flag in front of me while my United States Navy Senior Chief, Mike Seals, watched proudly with tears in his eyes.

Two months after the graduation ceremony, my cell phone rang. Mike called me many times a day, so I didn't think the call was going to be anything other than him saying hello and letting me know he was home from work. When I answered, though, Mike excitedly exclaimed, "Julie! Guess who I have here?"

"Ummmmm. Who?"

"Susan!" he almost shouted. Then he proclaimed, "Julie, I just told her that you and I are getting married—and soon! She wants to fly to Florida with us for our wedding. I want my daughter to be there. We're looking at plane tickets for all of us right now!"

"Oh, my gosh!" I responded.

"This is really happening?" I thought to myself.

We had talked about getting married multiple times a day, but it was suddenly getting REAL!

"Are you serious? You must be serious if you told Susan. And she's coming to the wedding?"

It may not have been the romantic scenario that some women long for, but it was exactly what it needed to be for Mike and me.

Mike's daughter had lost her mother to cancer only sixteen months earlier, and it had been understandably painful for her to see her dad find someone new to love so soon after their loss. Susan's approval was of tantamount importance to both Mike and me.

I had come to love Susan quickly, and it was extremely important to me that she was part of the process. Mike and I, along with Susan, her husband, and their baby daughter, were ALL flying to Florida to enjoy a couple of days of fun together after a small, intimate wedding. And I was ecstatic!

We made plans for our wedding to be held poolside in my cousin Kayla's backyard. I had slowly been reconnecting with some family members as God brought them back into my life, including my Uncle Bob (my mom's brother), his daughter, Kayla, and her husband, Mitch. They all believed in the change that had taken place in my life, and they absolutely loved Mike!

Both of my sisters had also come back into my life, which was an absolute miracle. I told them about the wedding and invited them, but they were not able to attend. I could tell they both had some trepidation as to whether or not our marriage would last, and I honestly understood how they could feel that way.

After all, my history with relationships was horrific, and I sensed they were both nervous and doubtful about me taking such a huge step in committing to marriage considering my track record. However, back then I didn't have the Lord living in me and through me. But both Mike and I had become Christian believers in love with Jesus, and because of THAT, I just knew we would have a wonderful, thriving marriage!

Before I knew it, our wedding day arrived. I slipped into the long, cream sundress that I had bought for the special occasion. As I gazed in a mirror that hung on the wall in the guest suite of Kayla and Mitch's beautiful Floridian home, I was struck by a powerful feeling of melancholy.

That day was truly bittersweet. My mom and dad were not alive. My dad would not be walking me down the aisle. I was very sad they didn't live to see that day. I again remembered the vision God gave me in my parents' upstairs bedroom that showed me in prison and one day being sober, happy, and free—but with the additional knowledge that neither of my parents would be alive to see it.

They would have loved Mike, because he is a good, responsible, funny, strong man who really loves me and treats me well. Even though my life growing up had been somewhat dysfunctional, I still loved my parents, and they always wanted to see me happy and successful. They would have been so proud of me being clean and sober, going to college, and marrying a good man.

I was stepping into a new season in my life, one I'd never imagined would be possible. I was about to become the wife of a United States Navy Senior Chief who was deeply in love and wanted to spend the rest of his life with me. The absolute goodness of God to have our marriage in His plan for me felt surreal. I was about to become Mrs. Julie Seals, the wife of a Christian man who loved Jesus just as deeply as I did.

I had finally made a good choice in a man, and I knew we were really going to have a wonderful marriage—a loving marriage, the marriage I had always dreamed of. My wedding day was going to be perfect! What could go wrong?

Then there was a knock at the front door, and my Uncle Bob arrived at the house with a case of champagne and hard liquor. Satan, it seemed, had other plans for my wedding. I looked aghast at him.

"Uncle Bob! I don't drink alcohol anymore!" I exclaimed.

"Well you do today! It's your wedding day!" he laughingly insisted.

We debated back and forth as he kept insisting that I at least had to toast my wedding with a glass of champagne. "Even one sip—it's tradition!" he affirmed.

I patiently but lovingly explained that as a former alcoholic and addict—and as a committed Christ-follower—I couldn't indulge in the very thing that had previously destroyed my life. Uncle Bob didn't understand, but he realized he wasn't going to talk me into drinking, even on my wedding day. So finally, he shrugged with resignation and gave up.

On that special day, Uncle Bob happily walked me down the small aisle next to Kayla and Mitch's sparkling pool. Mike's eyes were shining as he watched my approach. Then we exchanged our vows—for better or for worse, in sickness and in health, till death do us part! We promised to love Jesus Christ first, above the other, and to stay faithful to God and to one another.

In true Floridian style, the highlight of our wedding feast was fried gator tail with orange dipping sauce, and it was delicious. Later that afternoon, after we cut and ate the wedding cake, Mike whisked me off to the Inn at Cocoa Beach hotel for a glorious honeymoon and a couple of days of fun with Susan and her family.

I had no idea what lay ahead—growth, trials, ministry, pain, grief, and joy. For sure the future for us was not to be anything like the life I imagined. But it was everything God had planned—the future He planned for a purpose *much greater* than anything I could have dreamed up on my own!

THE START OF OUR MINISTRY

"Julie, there has got to be more to living for God than just going to church." Mike said to me.

We had been home from our honeymoon for two weeks, and we were just getting settled into married life in Temecula, California. We were going to church, but we both felt like something was missing. I looked at Mike, and I remembered the promise I made to God while I was in federal prison.

"There is more!" I responded. "Oh, Mike! There IS more!" Then I told him, "When I was in prison, I promised God that if He would let me out of prison, I'd spend the rest of my life going back IN to share the power and love and forgiveness of Jesus with inmates who are desperate for hope."

We had just started attending a new church, so we decided to approach the pastor the following Sunday. After the service, we excitedly asked Pastor Lewis if the church had a prison ministry. He said that while the church didn't have a prison ministry, he had recently met a woman, an ordained minister, who had just such a ministry called *God's Grace Ministries.*

Pastor Lewis was sure she would be willing to speak to us about our desire to go into prisons and minister to incarcerated women. He promised to get her name and number, and later that same day he called and gave us the information we needed to contact Reverend Christi Butler. And she turned out to be the first person God used to put Mike and me on the path He had planned all along for us to walk in together!

I immediately called Christi, introduced myself, and shared my story. She was very excited and let me know that she'd love it if I would accompany her into the minimum-security women's prison where she held a church service every Sunday morning. At the end of the conversation she asked if I would meet her for dinner that very evening so we could talk more about her ministry and added casually, "Why don't you bring your husband with you?"

When I asked Mike, he responded, "Sure! Why not? I haven't had dinner, and I don't have anything else to do."

That dinner changed our lives.

We met with Christi at a restaurant, and while enjoying a wonderful dinner, we talked and shared stories. Mike shared his testimony of his first wife dying of cancer and how her death broke his heart and brought him to the foot of the cross to surrender his life and heart to Jesus.

We were all wiping away tears of joy over the absolute goodness of God in each of our lives. Suddenly, Christi pulled out two sheets of paper from her purse and handed both Mike and me a Department of Corrections volunteer application that if accepted would allow us to go with her into Puerta La Cruz, a women's minimum security fire camp, and minister to female inmates who are trained to fight fires.

Christi explained that the prison had five fire trucks that were called out to fires in Southern California in the heat of the dry summers. Those female inmates, supervised by CAL FIRE staff, jumped on the fire trucks when the alarm went off and rushed to the scene of fires where they fought side-by-side with California's fire fighters.

In addition, she told us the inmates also provided extensive conservation and project services including sand bagging at local fire stations in San Diego County during the rainy seasons to help prevent flood damage. All their work facilitated the development of tangible skills and a strong work ethic that prepared them for successful integration back into the communities where they lived once they were released. I had never heard of a prison program like that, and it sounded so rewarding and productive.

I watched as Mike stared down at the application Christi laid down in front of him. "Me? You want *me* to fill one out too? I just came along for dinner," Mike explained with wonderment in his voice.

Later Mike shared with me that he didn't realize he would be able to minister in a women's prison with me. He thought he was just going to dinner for the food and the fellowship.

"Yes!" Christi announced with joy. "Fill it out! You can both come in with me!"

I glanced in wonder at Mike, and I saw a spark of excitement in his eyes that I had never seen before. Paul wrote to the church in Ephesus and told them,

> *For we are God's masterpiece. He has created us anew in Christ Jesus, so we can do the good things he planned for us long ago.* (Ephesians 2:10)

I didn't realize it at the time, but looking back, I now know beyond a shadow of a doubt that the spark in Mike's eyes marked the beginning of a deep inner awakening of his Ephesians 2:10 destiny.

What Paul wrote is beyond exciting! It means that God made me, Mike, and yes, YOU—you holding this book right now—as part of His masterpiece of creation. And He created each one of us with a special unique purpose. He has specific, exciting things for us to do, and those things were planned for us to do before we were even born!

We experience many things in life, and some of those things are full of pain and regret. But since God knows the future just as well as He knows the present and the past, He knew all those things would happen. And He still developed His plans for us.

His plans for us haven't changed, and today if we will surrender to God and allow Him to lead us into His amazing purpose for our lives, He will use each event of our lives to teach us, shape us, mold us, and prepare us for our destinies.

Mike and I took our applications home and filled them out that same night. And not long after submitting our background checks, a lieutenant from Puerta La Cruz called to let us know that Mike's application had been approved, but mine had not due to my criminal background.

I was crushed!

I explained to the lieutenant that I had given my life to Jesus, and after my release from prison I had enrolled in college and had earned my associate's degree with straight A's. I explained earnestly to the lieutenant that I was truly a changed person who wanted to come into his prison and tell the women all about Jesus. I reassured him that I was THE EXACT PERSON he *needed* to come in and share the life-transforming power of God with inmates who desperately needed to know there was hope and life after prison.

"I'm sorry," he replied with a business-like tone in his voice. "We can't let anyone come into this prison with a background as recent as yours." I know he could hear the disappointment in my voice, but he remained firm in his decision, said goodbye, and hung up.

I burst into tears!

"God, I don't understand! This is my dream. It's the dream YOU gave me, Lord. Oh God, please, PLEASE let him call me back! Please let them change their minds. Please let me go into prison, Lord!"

Mike turned from his computer, studied me for a moment, and said, "Pray, Julie. You pray. And then trust God."

"Okayyy," I sniffled as I tried to stop crying.

Mike's simple yet powerful reminder brought me back to a place of faith and prayer, and I began to pray earnestly for the Lord to open the doors so I could go into Puerta La Cruz and minister His love and power to the women incarcerated there.

Four days later, the same lieutenant called back again and asked to speak to me. All he said was, "Ms. Seals, you are approved to come into the prison."

"What!" I shouted out. "I'm APPROVED?"

"Yes," he replied, still with his business-like tone. "Have a nice day."

He hung up, and I screamed with joy!

With a mischievous smile, Mike said, "I told you so."

We both smiled, overjoyed at the prospect of going into a prison and ministering together as husband and wife—a TEAM for Jesus!

Reverend Christi (with whom we were becoming fast friends) put us on her ministry calendar to go into the prison with her and share our testimonies so the inmates could get to know us. We set our alarms for 5:00 am that next Sunday so we could get up and spend time in God's Word and prayer and share a pot of coffee.

With great excitement, we headed out the door at 6:30 am to make the two-hour drive from Temecula to Warner Springs, a remote wilderness area of San Diego County where the fire camp was nestled. We drove down the long winding single-lane road in awe of the majestic beauty of the forested landscape as well as the historic landmarks of old stagecoach stops.

I was nervous, but I also felt an enormous sense of purpose as we turned onto the long gravel road that led to the dusty dirt parking lot of the fire camp. I was apprehensive that the officers at the guard shack might not let me in—that my background might still be an issue even though the lieutenant had reassured me I had been approved. But, thankfully, my fears turned out to be unfounded.

Mike, Christi, and I gave our driver's licenses to the guard as we checked in and walked down a thin, cracked sidewalk to a building that housed an industrial-sized kitchen and a dining area with long tables and benches standing on a concrete floor. I learned the dining room doubled as the chapel, and we scurried to help Christi set up the sound system in preparation for our morning service.

Then the side door opened, and the women started to file in wearing faded and wrinkled orange prison uniforms. They carried their worn Bibles, and they all were eager to greet Christi and meet the new ministers (us!). Christi had a CD with worship songs that she played to begin the service, and I watched as all thirty-five women raised their hands to heaven and worshipped God with tears of joy streaming down their faces.

"This is where I belong!" I said to myself. "I belong doing ministry in a place where many in society have no desire to go—a place with people who have made mistakes and are considered outcasts—a place where people are desperate for the hope that can only be found in Jesus."

Christi introduced us, and Mike shared a brief ten-minute version of his testimony before handing the microphone to me. At the end of our testimonies, the women wept and were encouraged. We prayed with them at the end of the service, and they let us know how much it meant to them for us to take time out of our lives to visit them in prison.

Some very specific words of Jesus recorded by Matthew began to live in my heart that day.

> *Then the King will say to those on his right, "Come, you who are blessed by my Father, inherit the Kingdom prepared for you from the creation of the world. For I was hungry, and you fed me. I was thirsty, and you gave me a drink. I was a stranger, and you invited me into your home. I was naked, and you gave me clothing. I was sick, and you cared for me. I was in prison, and you visited me."*
>
> *Then these righteous ones will reply, "Lord, when did we ever see you hungry and feed you? Or thirsty and give you something to drink? Or a stranger and show you hospitality? Or naked and give you clothing? When did we ever see you sick or in prison and visit you?"*
>
> *And the King will say, "I tell you the truth, when you did it to one of the least of these my brothers and sisters, you were doing it to me!"* (Matthew 25:34-40)

As we started the drive home with tears of joy in our eyes, Mike and I were both overcome with the knowledge that WE were the ones more blessed by the ministry we had been privileged to take part in that morning!

And so, our journey as ministers of the hope and gospel of Jesus Christ began.

Chapter 15

JOURNEY TO THE PROMISED LAND

MIKE AND I were very happy together, and our work in the church and the women's prison was wonderful and spiritually fulfilling. But over time we began feeling restless. We were no longer happy in the Southern California environment and the increasing cost of living there. But most importantly, we felt God was calling us to move away from Temecula.

It's common for God to cause His children's spirits to feel restless prior to moving them into new chapters in their lives. And that was going on for a while before Mike looked at me one morning and suddenly proclaimed, "Let's move to Florida."

Without hesitation, I responded, "Okay! Let's do it!"

We had been together in Florida. We were married there, of course. And Florida was also where Mike grew up, so that seemed to be a sensible move for him. As for me though, there was a reason why moving so far away made no sense at all. It would place me on the opposite side of the nation as far from Tyler as I could possibly be.

I had received a legal judgment that allowed me to send monthly letters to Tyler. But before we decided to move, my letters to Tyler started coming back, stamped, "Return to Sender." (And I never knew if any were even read.) So by the time we decided to leave Temecula, I already realized his dad had moved and the lifeline connecting me to my son had already been broken.

Once again it felt like the Lord was saying to me, "It's not time yet, Julie. Just focus on me. Follow me!"

Mike and I both felt strongly that God was ordering our steps and sending us across the country even though we had no idea what He had in store. Miraculously, the United States Navy agreed to pay all expenses for our cross-country move even though it had been four years since Mike retired.

All U.S. Navy retirees are given one final, freebie move, but usually it must happen immediately upon retirement. Getting a free move four years later was unheard of. But one morning while in prayer, Mike heard the Lord speak to his heart and tell him to reach out and ask the Navy if they would consider reinstating his retirement move. And it was approved!

It was as if a spiritual red carpet was being placed at our feet, and the Lord himself was unrolling it to move us to a new place and season without giving us any of the details.

My little red Scion and Mike's blue Toyota Tacoma pickup were packed with our important personal documents, computers, and enough clothes for the four-day, cross-country trip. Interstate 10 would take us straight from Southern California to Jacksonville, Florida.

I had no idea what God had in store for us. I imagined that might be how a man named Abram felt when God told him to take his wife, Sarai, and his nephew, Lot, and leave his childhood home, friends, and all that was familiar so he could become *Abraham*, the father of many nations.

As recorded in the book of Genesis, God gave Abram orders to go to a land he knew nothing about, and He didn't provide him with a road map, a detailed action plan, or a set of goals and objectives. But Abram believed and obeyed God, and God gave him the new name of *Abraham*. Abraham became the father of Isaac, who became the father of Jacob—whose name was changed to *Israel*. And through the lineage of Israel, Jesus Christ, the Savior of the world—our Savior—was born!

Abram's willingness to surrender all and follow God was the key that opened the door to every promise God made to him. And I was learning (and still am) that being willing to surrender all to submit to God's guidance is the key that continues to open the door to the promises God has and continues to give to us.

God had given me many specific promises from His Word. Some of those promises had already come to pass. God had already prospered me and given me hope and a future (Jeremiah 29:11), but other promises had not yet come to pass—and more specifically, the promises that had to do with Tyler's salvation and the restoration of our relationship as mom and son.

God gave me these Scriptures to stand on:

> *"There is hope for your future," says the LORD.*
> *"Your children will come again to their own land."*
> (Jeremiah 31:17)

> *But the LORD says,*
> *"The captives of warriors will be released,*
> *and the plunder of tyrants will be retrieved.*
> *For I will fight those who fight you,*
> *and I will save your children."* (Isaiah 49:25)

Look and see, for everyone is coming home!
Your sons are coming from distant lands;
your little daughters will be carried home.
Your eyes will shine,
and your heart will thrill with joy . . . (Isaiah 60:4-5)

"Look around you and see,
for all your children will come back to you.
As surely as I live," says the Lord,
"they will be like jewels or bridal ornaments for you to display." (Isaiah 49:18)

I had no idea what the fulfillment of these Scriptures would look like as they played out in real life, but I remained fully convinced that God would somehow keep and fulfill these living, breathing promises that He had given to me.

THE PRAYER THAT CHANGED EVERYTHING

After moving to Florida and getting settled, Mike decided to take advantage of the GI bill and enroll in college. So he enrolled at Florida State College at Jacksonville and began pursuing an associate's degree.

Mike and I got up at 4:30 am every morning to read our Bibles, worship, and pray before starting the day. Then, after Mike left for college and I was all alone in our Floridian townhome, I would travail in noisy, wailing warfare prayer for my son's salvation—and for him to be fully restored to my life.

The Lord had led me to pray a very specific prayer over Tyler, and I prayed it over and over, every single morning.

Thank you, Father, that your Word says in 2 Peter 3:9 it is not your will for my son to perish but that your will for my son is for him to come to a saving knowledge of Jesus Christ!

Holy Spirit, I send you right now into Tyler's bedroom. You know exactly where he lives in California even though I don't. I don't know where they moved to or where his house is, but you do. Holy Spirit, fill Tyler's bedroom as he sleeps! Fill his entire bedroom, every molecule of the atmosphere, just like the train of the Lord's robe filled the temple in Isaiah 6:1.

Holy Spirit, I'm asking you to hover over Tyler and let your presence be so thick and so real that when Tyler opens up his eyes, he senses you—feels you—hovering right above him in his bed. And in that moment, as you are hovering above my son with your presence so thick and so real, I pray you will supernaturally fill my son with the knowledge that you created him, that you love him, that Jesus died to forgive him, and that you have a good plan for his life!

God, I pray this knowledge will cause him to weep and surrender his heart and life to you—right there in his bedroom!"

One morning as I finished my noisy warfare prayer, I walked over to my computer and pulled up Facebook. I had found Tyler on Facebook a few months earlier, but the Holy Spirit clearly told me not to reach out and send him a message or a friend request. I obeyed without question or reservation.

Tyler's Facebook page was set to "public," so I was able to see all his posts, and I could tell he was not a Christian living for Jesus. That morning there was a new picture on Tyler's

Facebook page of him playing water polo at his high school. I stared for a long time at the photograph of my teenage son as I wistfully remembered how much my four-year-old Tyler had loved his bath time.

I laughed quietly to myself, thinking of how he was always lying in the bottom of the bathtub and refusing to get out until every last drop of water had gone down the drain. Seeing his photo on the water polo team made me smile. And then something totally miraculous happened that I will never forget!

I clicked from Tyler's Facebook profile over to mine, and I started scrolling down through my posts and photos. I also had my profile set to public so if Tyler ever found me he could scroll through my posts and photos and get to know me from a distance and see that his momma was a transformed woman, deeply in love with Jesus, with a brand-new life.

I read through my Facebook posts in which I had expressed how much I missed Tyler and how deeply I regretted my past mistakes and longed for my little Tyler to come back into my life. And as I continued to scroll down through my profile, SUDDENLY, Tyler's pictures were there!

I saw posts he had written!

I shook my head and rubbed my eyes. Unbelievably, that morning my Facebook page and Tyler's Facebook page had totally merged. It was still my profile, but when I scrolled down, it became Tyler's photos and posts. The hair on my arms stood straight up as I grabbed my cell phone and started to video what I was seeing on my computer screen.

Awe and wonder filled my voice as I recorded and narrated the unbelievable miracle I was witnessing of my Facebook page and my son's Facebook page becoming ONE. There was *nothing but that* connecting me to Tyler that morning! He had no idea I was on Facebook and didn't know I had found his profile.

It was clear in my mind that God was speaking to me. Through the merging and blending together of our Facebook pages that morning, God was showing me that our lives were going to merge together again one day.

As I continued to monitor Tyler's Facebook posts and pray for him, I remained steadfast and faithful in my journey of letting God turn me into the woman, wife, sister, minister, and mother He had created me to become. In addition to Mike attending college, I had enrolled at the University of North Florida and was close to completing my second college degree to fulfill the promise I made to my mom.

The Lord again amazed me by making me the recipient of prestigious university and local community awards. I was honored by the mayor of the city of Jacksonville for giving up my Social Security Disability payments and stepping out into the workforce by getting a real full-time job for the first time in nineteen years.

I also won first place in a public speaking contest at the university. Me! The woman who at one point had been so strung out and high on meth that she couldn't speak a coherent sentence won first place in a public speaking competition at the University of North Florida!

TYLER COMES HOME

Two years passed from the day my Facebook page merged with Tyler's. Mike and I were attending the Peninsular Florida District School of Ministry to become credentialed ministers with the Assemblies of God when I began to see my son post things on his Facebook profile about God.

It was real what God was doing. In his self-proclaimed new life as a Christian, Tyler was giving up friendships that were not good! I was literally watching "*the substance of things hoped for*" and "*the evidence of things unseen*" (Hebrews 11:1 KJV) become a reality.

Whenever I saw those miracles on Tyler's Facebook page I would weep with gratitude, shout praise to God, and press into prayer harder than ever before. The miracle was coming, and it was coming soon.

When Tyler posted that he joined the Army and was heading to boot camp, I increased my prayers for his inner healing and protection. One of the Scriptures I had been praying over Tyler for years was Psalm 147:3: "*He heals the brokenhearted and bandages their wounds.*" And God showed me He was moving powerfully in my son's heart in response to my fervent, unceasing prayers when, at boot camp, Tyler posted a picture of a new vertical tattoo cascading down his entire left shoulder blade.

The tattoo said, *Love Defeated Hate*, and the comment he added to the post read, "Signification of the day the Lord finally freed me from the pain of my past. So grateful!"

Through the open window I had into Tyler's life given to me through the blessing of social media, I learned he dedicated the tattoo to me, and it represented the day the Lord helped him to forgive me for failing him so greatly when he was a little boy.

Mike and I prayed, and we both felt a release from God.

It was time!

The Lord was finally allowing me to reach out to Tyler!

I asked Mike to help me figure out exactly where Tyler's boot camp was. Then, we set out for the Navy Commissary to buy candy, chips, and other snacks to put in a care package to send to Tyler. I also bought a small, leather Bible with the official seal and emblem of the United States Department of the Army on the cover. Hands trembling, I wrote Tyler a note, keeping it short because I didn't want to overwhelm him.

> Dear Tyler, I hope you like this Bible and these snacks. I want you to know how truly sorry I am for all the mistakes I made all those years ago. I am a Christian now and I love Jesus. I love you SO much and I pray for you every single day! I also pray that one day you will find it in your heart to forgive me and that you will want to see me. In case you are curious, my Facebook name is, Julie Fitzpatrick Seals. I love you, Tyler! With all my love—Mom!

Three months later, with my heart almost beating out of my chest, Mike drove me to the Jacksonville International Airport. I could barely contain my excitement! Tyler and I had been communicating over the phone, and the day had finally come when he was ready to see me. My son, my Tyler, wanted to see his momma!

Every Scripture, every promise, and every word of knowledge that God had ever given to me about Tyler flooded the forefront of my mind as we walked (okay, I almost ran) through the airport terminal to meet my son.

Tyler's dad and I had just spoken on the phone earlier that morning, and we had come to a place of peace and forgiveness. I was able to apologize from my heart for the pain my past actions had caused. The unfathomable, powerful MERCY of God was touching every soul involved.

God's limitless grace was woven throughout every human dynamic of the miracles we were experiencing. The Lord was leaving nothing undone!

With every step I took through the airport terminal, my heart was echoing Jeremiah 31:16-17—the Scripture passage God gave me when I was in prison to pray and stand on in faith for that very moment in time. And I write it here again:

> *But now this is what the Lord says:*
> *"Do not weep any longer,*
> *for I will reward you," says the Lord.*
> *"Your children will come back to you*
> *from the distant land of the enemy.*
> *There is hope for your future," says the Lord.*
> *"Your children will come again to their own land."*

I stood on my tip toes to peer down the long corridor at the passengers rolling their carry-on bags behind them as they headed toward waiting family members. God was watching over His Word to perform it, like He promised Jeremiah.

> *And the Lord said, "That's right, and it means that I am watching, and I will certainly carry out all my plans."*
> (Jeremiah 1:12)

Suddenly, Mike said, "LOOK! Julie. That's him! There he is! GO!"

While Tyler was still a long way off, I started toward him, smiling all the way. The knife-like, agonizing pain I had felt searing my heart for fifteen years was replaced with indescribable joy! I ran the last few steps toward Tyler as he dropped his duffle bag to embrace me—with ARMS WIDE OPEN!

EXCEEDINGLY, ABUNDANTLY, ABOVE AND BEYOND

"Look around you and see,
for all your children will come back to you.
As surely as I live," says the Lord,
"they will be like jewels or bridal ornaments for you to display." (Isaiah 49:18)

Never in a million years could I have imagined *the way* God would bring His Word in Isaiah 49:18 to pass. When the Lord gave me this Scripture during my twenty-two-month stay in federal prison, He simply imparted to me a *knowing* that I must stand on *this* Specific promise (among the many others He gave me). And He promised me I would live to see this very Scripture come alive in my life.

At first, I imagined it meant Tyler would come back into my life. We would be reunited—period—The End. After all, wasn't that enough? Wasn't that the miracle of miracles? But Ephesians 3:20 says that God is *"able, through his mighty power at work within us, to accomplish infinitely more than we might ask or think."*

One of the first questions I had for Tyler during his first visit to Florida was how he got saved. "Tell me how you got saved!" I told him, "How did you come to give your life to Jesus?"

I won't go into the details here in this book, because Tyler has his own story to tell. But I will say that God met my son right there in his bedroom, like I prayed for so many years. Everything I asked the Lord to do for my son, He DID!

Then God did far more than I even dared to ask when one year after his first visit to see me, Tyler packed his little blue Honda Civic and drove from California to Florida to live with Mike and me.

I would be lying if I said the rest of our story has been a walk in the park. Family life is challenging and messy, whether it is a blended family or not. But God has carried us all, faithfully, through every hard moment, and He has blessed us with so many wonderful memories—memories that to this day are still being made. He truly is a good, good Father!

A GEORGIA WEDDING

The sun shone brilliantly in the sky, creating the perfect lighting for an outdoor barn wedding. I had never seen Tyler look so handsome. Mike was the minister officiating the ceremony at the request of both Tyler and his wife. Both of my sisters, their husbands, and their children were there to celebrate with us.

As the music began to play, I stepped forward and smiled up at Tyler, who was holding out his arm to me.

"Come on, mom! You ready?"

There I was, walking my son down the aisle on his wedding day so he could marry the woman of his dreams. I lifted up my eyes and looked around, taking in every incredible detail. I was almost faint from the joy that comes with being a mom in a moment like that.

"I am loved! I'm surrounded by family!" were my thoughts. "I have what I always longed for but could never grasp until my heart and life were centered on and fully surrendered to Jesus Christ!"

God has done far more in my life than I could ever dare to ask or even dream of. He has gone infinitely beyond my highest prayers, desires, thoughts, and hopes. When the heavy metal doors to that federal prison slammed shut behind me, I thought my life was over. But it wasn't.

It was only the beginning. God is *still* writing my story. There's so much more coming.

THE HOPE DEALER

Gone is my life as an addict. Gone are the days when I stole from others to support my habit. Gone are the days when I ran from reality. And gone are the days when I consumed anything I could find to dull my pain by clouding my brain.

Gone are the days when I lived in seeming hopelessness. Gone are my days as a failed parent. Gone are the days when I lived in spiritual darkness and allowed myself to be mistreated and overcome by the enemy. And gone are the days when I was a drug dealer for the man.

Welcome to my new life. Welcome to today! Welcome to the new identity God has given to me. Welcome to my life now as a HOPE Dealer for Jesus!

God took my old life—a life broken for so many years—and made it new. God took all my years consumed by hopeless feelings and replaced them with years inspired by hope, empowered by love, and bursting with expectations of even more in the future.

God never forgot about me, and regardless of what you've been thinking, He has not forgotten about you! He not only sees you where you are—and as you are—*right now*, He also understands you completely.

God proved His love to me by pursuing me relentlessly and revealing himself to me step by step over many years—even when I ran from Him—and I assure you He is doing that for you right now. Will you open your heart and receive it?

God saved me, filled me with His Holy Spirit, tutored me in His patience, and taught me what I needed to enable me to live then, now, and into the future with an unwavering Hope.

I know He will do for you what He did for me . . . if you allow Him to do it.

We're all different, with different life experiences. But God knows about all of them. He knew how to speak to me in ways I could hear Him. And He knows how to speak to you.

That's what He wants to do. He wants to speak to you and deliver you from your past, acquaint you with His love, and launch you into the future as another new creation in Him—a new life filled with great potential and unlimited hope.

Even when I was still in prison, I became free in Jesus. Even behind the concertina wire looking out, in my spirit I was a prisoner no more. Even behind bars, God filled me with hope. And now I continue to confess with joy, Jesus is All My HOPE! And He wants to be yours too.

Let Him!

EPILOGUE

As of this writing in late 2022, Mike and I have been married over sixteen years, and I'm glad to say we're not simply head over heels in love with each other as husband and wife; we're the very best of friends and partners in ministry! And our passion and commitment to the kingdom of God is unwavering and relentless.

In December of 2017, Tyler and his wife, Laura, had a precious baby girl. They named her Charlotte. So Mike and I are grandparents! OH, CAN SOMEBODY PRAISE THE LORD? He is GOOD! He restores. He redeems. He is faithful. His timing is perfect. And His plans far exceed our wildest dreams!

Mike and I are now Ordained Ministers with the Assemblies of God. And you should understand after reading our testimonies that God took two people from entirely different backgrounds—yet both utterly hopeless—joined them together, and said, "Now, go forth and feed my sheep! Love my people! Help the hurting, the lost, and the hopeless!"

God takes prisoners and makes them prison ministers. God takes drug addicts like the old Julie and turns them into college graduates and fire-filled evangelists. God takes angry husbands like the old Mike and transforms them into faith-filled, humble, compassionate leaders of their homes. Then He sends them out on His mission to reach a lost and hurting world!

Isaiah 61:1 says, *"The Spirit of the Sovereign Lord is upon me, for the Lord has anointed me to bring good news to the poor. He has sent me to comfort the brokenhearted and to proclaim that captives will be released and prisoners will be freed."*

Isaiah was writing of the coming Messiah, but these words also describe the activities that followers of Christ are meant to be involved in. And that's because we believers have been charged with being the fleshly representatives of Jesus on earth, and we are being empowered by the Holy Spirit to carry on the works of Jesus until He returns.

God's love has not ended, and His work in our lives is not finished. He continues to amaze us with the greatness of His love and the enormity of His marvelous grace.

Mike is now a Florida Department of Corrections Senior Chaplain. I'm an Evangelist, a prison minister, and author. And I have also been blessed to be called on to represent Jesus to many people as a conference speaker.

In January of 2022, I co-founded *Her Hope Recovery Ministry* in Lake City, Florida. As part of that ministry I co-host a Christ-centered, online, 12-step recovery meeting for women every week and gather local women in recovery together for a monthly breakfast club.

God is moving powerfully among these women, and they are being discipled as they fall in love with Jesus, receive the baptism of the Holy Spirit, and regain custody of their children.

FOR MORE INFORMATION or to learn about how you can become a ministry partner with me, please visit my website. Also, did this book help you in some way? If so, I would love to hear about it. You can write to me at my ministry address found on the *Contact* page of **JulieSeals.com.**